EVERYDAY COOK

For Oliver:
Thanks for your big adventurous appetite and
keeping us cooking every day!

EVERYDAY COOK

VIBRANT RECIPES, SIMPLE METHODS, DELICIOUS DISHES

HODDER &
STOUGHTON

Donal Skehan

First published in Great Britain in 2021 by Hodder & Stoughton
An Hachette UK company

2

A CIP catalogue record for this title is available from the British Library

Hardback ISBN 978 1 529 36892 5
eBook ISBN 978 1 529 36894 9

Executive Publisher: Liz Gough
Project Editor: Isabel Gonzalez-Prendergast
Editorial Assistant: Olivia Nightingall
Design: Evi-O. Studio | Evi O. & Nicole Ho
Copyeditor: Clare Sayer
Food photography: Donal Skehan
Lifestyle photography: Kate Dowling
Cover Photography: Evan Doherty
Food and Props Stylist: Sarah-Kim Watchorn
Food Assistant: Susan Willis
Senior Production Controller: Diana Talyanina

Colour origination by Born Group
Printed and bound in Germany by Mohn Media

Hodder & Stoughton policy is to use papers that are natural, renewable
and recyclable products and made from wood grown in sustainable
forests. The logging and manufacturing processes are expected to
conform to the environmental regulations of the country of origin.

Hodder & Stoughton Ltd
Carmelite House
50 Victoria Embankment
London
EC4Y 0DZ

www.hodder.co.uk

Follow Donal at @donalskehan on Twitter and Instagram and at
/donalskehan on Facebook and YouTube.
www.donalskehan.com

INTRODUCTION

A BLUEPRINT OF RECIPES

The push and pull on our busy lives means that the routine of cooking a decent home-cooked meal can often find itself being pushed down our list of priorities. Reclaiming our kitchens without sacrificing our time is possibly one of the most important things we can do for ourselves and for family life. Finding time during the day to mull over a slow-blipping pot of stew or giving yourself the gift of well-prepared ingredients that can be transformed into a simple yet satisfying hearty dinner is a true tonic to a whole manner of weekly woes. Over the past few years my life has had plenty of twists and turns, moving across the world and adding children to the mix, but now that I'm back home and closer to my family I see the importance of those essential recipes that make our home kitchen tick, the classic dishes we come back to time and time again for comfort and security. Despite the pressure on time life provides, cooking and eating together remains one of my favourite things to do. In this book, I want to provide you with a blueprint of recipes that will allow you to manage the madness life throws at you AND get a supper to the table that everyone wants to devour. A nourishing bowl of home-cooked food is one of the most overlooked balms for yourself and your loved ones.

Quick cooking has become a prerequisite for feeding our family and a staple part of our weekly routine. But dishes that are quick to prep, yet slow to cook also play a part too. Recipes that don't require long lists of ingredients, dishes that don't leave a mountain of washing-up and time-saving tricks that bring seriously great flavour to the table are the most important part of making everyday favourites with ease.

ADOPT A MEAL-PREP MINDSET

It's safe to say that most households face the same old question when supper rolls around: 'What's for dinner?' In this book you will find the answer: comfort food classics and simple everyday favourites, one-pot wonders brought steaming straight to the table and fast feasts that take less than 15 minutes from kitchen to plate but that are still big on vibrant flavour. Adopt a meal-prep mindset to make your kitchen work for you, with recipes that you can make ahead of time to keep or freeze. This way you can keep your family well nourished from Monday to Friday and through the weekend, where baking classics will come into their own.

The recipes themselves are here to make life easy. Doable dinners like the creamy Brussels sprouts pasta with zesty pangrattato or dark and unctuous hoisin shredded duck with plenty of fresh veggies to wrap it up with will bring fast flavour even if you're just in the door from work. Home comfort classics like my Irish shepherd's pie with a light and fluffy champ potato mash topping or the creamy chicken and broccoli pie with a cheesy cobbler topping will be worth the wait. And spicy peanut butter satay pork or deep, dark and delicious roast vegetable tagine can happily lie in wait in your fridge or freezer for your hungry dinner needs in the Make & Freeze chapter.

MAKE YOUR KITCHEN WORK FOR YOU

The key to this cookbook is to celebrate those everyday classic-cooking recipes that will help your kitchen work for you. As a food writer I am constantly looking for new ideas and recipe inspiration but, if I'm honest, having reliable recipes that I can easily whip up are what I most come back to and make time after time. The meal planning guide will help you lay out a week of good eating and cooking, proving that a well-maintained kitchen will save you money, reduce food waste and ultimately feed you with delicious dinners.

I think the wish of anyone who writes cookbooks is that their books become dog-eared, sauce-splattered, well-used guides to the kitchen, and that is exactly why I want to share with you the recipes that make our kitchen tick, spark joy and ultimately leave our bellies full without the fuss. I hope they become regular additions to your weekly cooking routine and find a place at the table for birthdays, dinners with friends and whatever life throws your way.

MEAL PLANS

As I've written about in previous cookbooks, one of the key aspects that helps our family kitchen to function well is meal plans, so much so that recently I've designed an online platform dedicated to them. I used to spend hours organising the weekly meal plan with recipes and shopping lists, but with Donal's Kitchen (donalskitchen.com), the process is automated: you simply click the recipes you want to cook for the week and a shopping list is automatically created. This book is filled with plenty of recipes ideal for both meal planning or indeed meal prepping. Whether you are a seasoned home-cooking pro or a novice just starting out, I want to provide you with a guide on how to kick-start your kitchen with everyday recipes that will fill you with kitchen confidence. Overleaf you'll find a month's worth of meal plans with tips and shopping lists to get you started cooking recipes from this book.

SOME NOTES ON MEAL PLANNING...

Before we go any further, particularly if you are someone who is rolling your eyes at the thought of such structure being applied to cooking, let me just say that meal planning is not for everyone and should certainly not become another thing you have to worry about on your to-do list. Like most home cooks, I love the freedom and spontaneity of shopping for seasonal vegetables, picking up something exciting from the butcher or discovering a new ingredient or cooking technique, which meal planning doesn't necessarily always allow for.

What it does provide, however, is reliability for busy households; it removes the guesswork from dinner time, which for many families can be a stressful moment in the day. In our house, we certainly don't use a meal plan all the time but when we do it's often to help the flow of a busy week and to avoid having any kitchen mealtime meltdowns. There will always be time for a slow Saturday morning, plodding around the kitchen with coffee dreaming up what to make for a weekend feast but midweek, when dinner needs to be on the table, I want to be armed with the ingredients and a plan.

The true success of a good weekly meal plan comes down to three key elements: variety of flavours, ease of recipes and flexibility. With this in mind when I arrange my weekly meal plans I like to choose a good variety of different recipes, including veg-forward meals, chicken dinners, devourable pasta suppers or something big on flavour and texture, so that each night feels different and you have something to look forward to rather than the prospect of a daily chore.

My recipe writing has changed in recent years to reflect the demands of becoming a new parent and recipes that are an instant success are always a winner, particularly when it comes to meal planning. It's also important to consider what you choose for your meal plan – save the homemade dumplings, lasagne or the outdoor barbecue project for the weekend. On a busy weeknight the recipes should really take less than 30 minutes to cook or prep. Lastly, flexibility is key. We all know that our best-laid plans can quickly unravel as the week unfolds, so the ability to roll with the punches and move things around as needed is essential; just because you have a meal plan does not mean you are tied to it. Ingredients can be frozen, dinners can be transformed to lunches and there's always room to change things around so please approach meal planning with this flexible mindset.

There are recipes for every aspect of life in the kitchen in this book but for this monthly meal plan I want to highlight some of the ones I feel are easiest and most doable for your midweek cooking. Things I look for in a recipe when I'm meal planning are a shorter ingredients list, a recipe that doesn't require too long a cooking time and one that doesn't need too much equipment. Once you've laid out the recipes for the week, the shopping list is next. Write it in order of how you would shop – fruit and vegetables, dairy, meat and fish, store cupboard, frozen – this will prevent you from zigzagging across the store and make your shopping more efficient.

STREAMLINING YOUR COOKING EXPERIENCE

When you get your weekly shop home, unpack with cooking in mind. Clear out old ingredients to use up first and start fresh by doing any small tasks like washing vegetables, removing packaging or putting ingredients in their own containers – this will all go a long way to streamlining your cooking experience when the time comes. Many of the recipes here will also have plenty of items that can be made up on a Sunday before the week starts, minimising the amount you have to do at dinner time. Grains can be cooked and stored, salad dressings made and sealed in jars, veggies shredded or meats marinated. Even just 15 minutes on a Sunday night can help you get in the zone and ready for the week ahead.

WEEK ONE

MONDAY

Chicken & Cheddar
Cobbler Pie p. 128

TUESDAY

Chickpea, Tomato
& Lentil Soup with
Spiced Oil p. 183

WEDNESDAY

No Rise, No Fuss
One-pan Pizza p. 65

THURSDAY

Creamy Brussels
Sprouts Pasta p. 48

FRIDAY

Crispy Hoisin
Duck Lettuce
Wraps p. 52

SHOPPING LIST

VEGETABLES & FRUIT

- 1–2 carrots
- 150g (5oz) purple sprouting broccoli
- 100g (3½oz) baby spinach
- 1 large onion
- 400g (14oz) fresh tomatoes
- 125g (4oz) king oyster mushrooms
- 1 courgette (zucchini)
- 200g (7oz) Brussels sprouts
- 2 heads of baby gem lettuce
- ½ cucumber
- 4 spring onions (scallions)
- 1 red chilli
- 1 lemon
- 5cm (2in) piece of fresh ginger
- Garlic
- Dill
- Coriander (cilantro)
- Thyme
- Flat-leaf parsley

MEAT, POULTRY & FISH

- 1 rotisserie chicken
- 200g (7oz) diced pancetta
- 4 confit duck legs

STORE CUPBOARD

- Plain flour
- 500g (4 cups) 00 flour
- Baking powder
- 475g (3¾ cups) self-raising flour
- 400g (14oz) orecchiette
- 125g (4oz) pickled pearl onions
- 200ml (¾ cup) passata
- 125g (4oz) jarred artichoke hearts in oil
- 400g (14oz) tin chickpeas
- 250g (9oz) pack ready-cooked green or puy lentils
- 500ml (2 cups) chicken stock
- 600ml (2½ cups) vegetable stock
- Dijon mustard
- Ground cumin
- Cumin seeds
- Ground turmeric
- Coriander seeds
- Chinese five-spice
- Sesame seeds
- Chilli flakes
- Honey
- Dark soy sauce
- Light soy sauce
- Hoisin sauce

FRIDGE

- 150ml (5fl oz) single cream
- Crème fraîche
- 300g (10oz) butter
- Natural yoghurt
- 100g (3½oz) Irish Cheddar
- 250g (9oz) grated mozzarella
- 125g (4oz) ball buffalo mozzarella
- Parmesan cheese
- 100g (3½oz) fresh white breadcrumbs

WEEK TWO

MONDAY

Prawn & Basil
Stir Fry p. 46

TUESDAY

Mac 'n' Peas p. 143

WEDNESDAY

Quick-Fix Saucy
Pantry Chicken p. 32

THURSDAY

Crispy Egg Fried
Rice Bowls p. 138

FRIDAY

Charred Lamb
Kebabs with Pickled
Onions & Saffron
Yoghurt p. 98

SHOPPING LIST

VEGETABLES & FRUIT

- 1 large cauliflower
- 250g (9oz) tenderstem broccoli
- 6 spring onions (scallions)
- 1 carrot
- 2 red onions
- 2 red Thai chillies
- 2 red chillies
- 1 lime
- 1 lemon
- Garlic
- Basil
- Coriander (cilantro)
- Mint
- Flat-leaf parsley

MEAT, POULTRY & FISH

- 16–20 large raw prawns (jumbo shrimp)
- 8 rashers of smoked streaky bacon
- 8 free-range skinless chicken thigh fillets
- 800g (1lb 12oz) lamb leg

STORE CUPBOARD

- Plain flour
- Caster sugar
- 4 large free-range eggs
- 350g (12oz) macaroni
- 250g (9oz) jasmine or basmati rice
- 4 large pitta breads
- 30g (1oz) pine nuts
- 400ml (14fl oz) vegetable stock
- 150ml (5fl oz) white wine
- 100ml (3½fl oz) groundnut (peanut) oil
- Sesame oil
- Capers
- Fish sauce
- Soy sauce
- Rice vinegar
- Dijon mustard
- Honey
- Hot sauce
- Oyster sauce
- Sesame seeds
- Ras el hanout
- Saffron
- Coriander seeds

FRIDGE

- Unsalted butter
- 200g (7oz) Greek yoghurt
- 100g (3½oz) mascarpone
- Parmesan cheese
- 75g (3oz) grated mozzarella
- 225g (8oz) firm tofu
- 200g (7oz) hummus
- 325g (11oz) frozen peas

Week Three

MONDAY

Mee Goreng p. 80

TUESDAY

One-Pan Chicken
Saltimbocca
with Courgettes
& Tenderstem p. 79

WEDNESDAY

Creamy Coconut
& Lemongrass
Fish Stew p. 56

THURSDAY

Smoky Chicken
Taco Night p. 104

FRIDAY

Korean-style
Sloppy Sliders p. 106

SHOPPING LIST

VEGETABLES & FRUIT

- Spring onions (scallions)
- 2 pak choi or choi sum
- 300g (3½oz) green beans
- 4 red onions
- 400g (14oz) red-skinned potatoes
- 200g (7oz) cherry tomatoes
- 2 courgettes (zucchini)
- 200g (7oz) tenderstem broccoli
- Beansprouts
- Baby spinach
- ¼ red cabbage
- 1 large avocado
- 1 large carrot
- ½ cucumber
- 1 green finger chilli
- 2 long red chillies
- Garlic
- 5 limes
- 4 lemongrass stalks
- Sage
- Mint
- Thai basil
- Coriander

MEAT, POULTRY & FISH

- 200g (7oz) raw king prawns (jumbo shrimp)
- 500g (1lb 2 oz) firm white fish
- 4 small free-range chicken breasts
- 750g (1lb 10oz) free-range skinless chicken thigh fillets
- 8 slices of prosciutto
- 500g (1lb 2oz) minced (ground) beef (15% fat)

STORE CUPBOARD

- Soft light brown sugar
- Soft dark brown sugar
- 250g (9oz) Thai jasmine long grain rice
- 12 brioche slider burger buns
- 6 large flour or corn tortillas
- 100ml (3½fl oz) white wine
- Groundnut (peanut) oil
- Sesame oil
- 400ml (14fl oz) tin coconut milk
- 200ml (¾ cup) vegetable stock
- Kecap manis
- Soy sauce
- Ketchup
- Fish sauce
- Sambal oelek
- Thai fish sauce
- Rice wine vinegar
- Sriracha
- Star anise
- Mayonnaise
- Medium curry powder
- Ground cumin
- Chipotle powder
- Sesame seeds

FRIDGE

- 225g (8oz) firm tofu
- 300g (10oz) fresh egg noodles
- Guacamole

WEEK FOUR

MONDAY

Chicken Piccata p. 39

TUESDAY

Veggie-packed Yuk Sung p. 130

WEDNESDAY

Cheat's Spring Risotto with Orzo, Mint & Courgette p. 36

THURSDAY

Spicy Prawn Aglio e Olio p. 154

FRIDAY

Kung Pao Chicken & Aubergine p. 164

SHOPPING LIST

VEGETABLES & FRUIT

- 200g (7oz) green beans
- Baby leaf spinach
- 2 carrots
- 300g (10oz) oyster or shitake mushrooms
- Spring onions (scallions)
- 2–3 baby gem lettuces
- 2 aubergines (eggplants)
- 1 red (bell) pepper
- 2 large courgettes (zucchini)
- 225g (8oz) water chestnuts
- 1 small onion
- 1 red chilli
- 3 lemons
- Garlic
- Ginger
- Flat-leaf parsley
- Coriander
- Lemon thyme
- Mint
- Basil

MEAT, POULTRY & FISH

- 4 free-range chicken breasts
- 8 free-range skinless chicken thigh fillets
- 500g (1lb 2oz) raw king prawns (jumbo shrimp)

STORE CUPBOARD

- Plain flour
- Cornflour
- 400g (14oz) linguini
- 100g (3½oz) vermicelli noodles
- 350g (12oz) orzo pasta
- 400g (14oz) spaghetti
- Rice
- 200ml (¾ cup) white wine
- 750ml (3 cups) vegetable or chicken stock
- Groundnut (peanut) oil
- Sesame oil
- 4 anchovies in oil
- Capers
- Chinese five-spice
- Soy sauce
- Honey
- Rice wine vinegar
- Shaoxing rice wine
- Chilli flakes
- Peanuts

FRIDGE

- Unsalted butter
- Parmesan cheese
- 400g (14oz) quorn mince
- 100g (3½oz) frozen peas
- 125ml (½ cup) double (heavy) cream
- 65g (2½oz) pecorino

RECLAIMING OUR KITCHENS
WITHOUT SACRIFICING OUR TIME
IS POSSIBLY ONE OF THE MOST
IMPORTANT THINGS WE CAN DO
FOR OURSELVES AND FOR FAMILY LIFE.

SIMPLE THINGS THAT WILL CHANGE HOW YOU COOK

Confidence in the kitchen is the best tool you can arm yourself with. Unfortunately it doesn't come after cooking one dish well; instead it gradually grows on you after years of trial and error, kitchen blunders and successfully served suppers. All of a sudden you find yourself less consumed by following a recipe's instructions to the letter and instead a well-cooked meal is produced through an understanding of the basic principles of flavour and the simple, small techniques and finishing touches that set really good home-cooked meals apart. Even if you are an established cook there is always something to be learned in the kitchen and a well-tested recipe will be interpreted by whoever cooks it and will almost always provide varying results. For this reason, I want to lean in to some of the things that really do make a difference to how you cook and serve your food. I've watched and read countless messages from people who have been cooking my recipes for years now; often it can be something as simple as having the pan hot enough before searing meat, using the best-quality ingredients or getting into the habit of tasting at the different stages of cooking that can make a significant improvement to the final dish and your cooking in general.

Beyond cooking skills, having a kitchen that is well organised is the cornerstone of great cooking. I say this as much to myself as to you reading this, as I am certainly guilty of shoving ingredients to the back of the kitchen cupboard and closing the door, allowing vegetables to wither in the bottom of the fridge and filling my drawers with utensils and gadgets that are not always necessary. As much as my scattered mind may protest, my best cooking comes from a clean, well-organised kitchen. Having the right utensils, mixing bowls, frying pans and chopping knives can completely change your cooking, and having them to hand will transform your experience in the kitchen.

ORGANISE YOUR KITCHEN SYSTEM

Cooking great food is one thing but having a system in place in which to do it is another. It can easily be achieved and is a good starting point, whether you are a novice in the kitchen or a seasoned pro looking to shake things up. Here are a few things that help our kitchen tick.

An initial clear-out of ingredients is essential if you want to start fresh. Take everything out of the cupboards, check best before dates, only put ingredients you are going to use back in and top up on regular everyday ingredients.

Kitchen tools – look at what you have and purge any kitchen gadgets, utensils or bulky items that don't get used regularly. Everything you need should be visible where possible and easy to grab while you cook. Kitchen shelving and hooks are easy to install and will save you time spent rooting through drawers.

Consider upgrading some of your kitchen kit. Kitchen gadgets you SHOULD spend money on include kitchen knives, wooden chopping boards, a good pepper mill, a digital instant-read meat thermometer and a hand-held blender. Go to a good kitchen supply shop and stock up on utensils that work for you.

Kitchen Tips

Lay out a designated cooking station – this should include a jar of key utensils such as tongs, a rubber spatula, wooden spoons, etc. Fill a jar with forks and spoons and use them to regularly taste food or measure or flip ingredients. I also keep a little trug next to where I chop with oils, vinegars, salt and pepper and anything else I use regularly.

Label everything – keep a roll of masking tape and some pens or markers close to hand so you can label leftovers before they fall into the depths of the freezer and label shelves or drawers. It's something so simple but instantly takes the guesswork out of time in the kitchen.

Organise your ingredients – dividing your ingredients into sections in baskets or boxes within your kitchen shelves can make life a lot easier. Asian staples, labelled spices, pasta shapes, grains and dried pulses will all be much easier to lay your hands on if they are grouped and stored together. Similarly, decanting staple ingredients like flour and sugar into glass or clear plastic containers will allow you to see what you have without the guesswork. If you can't see it clearly when you open your cupboard doors, it's likely you'll forget it's there and won't use it. The same can be done in the fridge: group items together and keep a section for leftovers. Regular rotation will help to avoid a black hole at the back of the fridge, freezer or kitchen cupboard.

Organise your utensils – stacking ten bowls on top of each other might be the easiest option when unpacking the dishwasher but ensuring your utensils are on the path of least resistance will provide easy access. Ideally you want bowls for prep in easy reach, utensils in their place and frying pans that can go straight from a shelf or cupboard to stovetop without having to wrestle them out from under a pile of other pans.

Everything should have a place and be in its place. Organise items for food preparation, cooking, serving and storing all in separate cupboards or drawers. This will streamline your kitchen flow while cooking.

Stock up on reusable containers– they are the lifeblood of my fridge and freezer. They are great for storing leftovers, using for meal preparation and for marinating meats.

Reorganise regularly, make it part of your monthly schedule. Start a new month of cooking afresh with a fridge clear-out, a cupboard reorganisation and a purge of anything that no longer serves your cooking needs.

COOK FOR SUCCESS

PREP

How you prepare your ingredients for a recipe can be the makings of a successful meal. Lay out the ingredients you need before you start. A little *mise en place* while you cook is what separates the novice from the pro. Keep to hand prep bowls and pull them out every time you start cooking. One for scraps, one for ingredients and one for prepped and ready-to-go ingredients. It's a simple habit but really does help to keep your cooking streamlined.

Clean as you go while you're in the zone. At times I'm certainly guilty of leaving a trail of destruction in the kitchen as I cook but more often than not, when I'm at my best in the kitchen, I will put away ingredients no longer needed, wash utensils by hand or stack the dishwasher while a sauce bubbles or pasta cooks. It makes for easier cooking and ultimately an easier clean-up once everyone has eaten.

Prep really comes into its own, however, when you make a double batch of a recipe as you're already spending time in the kitchen – two meals for the 'price' of one if you like! And when there are mouths to feed, you can make life easier for yourself by multitasking; if you're going to stick on the oven or light up the hob, you may as well use it. Rice or pasta can be cooked, eggs can be boiled, a tray of vegetables roasted, garlic mayo or a quick salad dressing jar whizzed together while you're at the chopping board.

COOK

There are many techniques to really master individual recipes but there are a few simple tips that are often overlooked. I urge you to pay attention to these as you cook through the recipes in this book as it will really help you to master them.

1   Cooking at the right heat. Whether it's meat, fish or vegetables, the difference between searing and sweating is huge. Not having your pan hot enough before you start cooking on it is one of the biggest mistakes I see. As soon as you add an ingredient to the pan it brings down the temperature, so if it's sizzle you're after it's important to make sure the pan is really hot. Take the time to get this right and it will help develop flavour in your cooking. Also, don't be tempted to prematurely move ingredients in the pan – allow them to develop that rich colour.

2   Taste as you go. This is an obvious one but it really does make a difference to the final meal to taste at each stage. Even if you forget, taste before you serve and adjust the seasoning as needed.

3   Bring meat to room temperature before cooking and pat dry with kitchen paper to remove as much liquid as possible – this will help you get that rich brown colour and prevent it from sweating in the pan.

4   Pay more attention to the look of ingredients as they cook rather than the time in recipe instructions. This one is key as oven and pan temperatures will vary. If it's a caramelised brown colour on onion frying that you are looking for, or crisp and golden vegetables roasting in a tray, you may need to cook for more – or less – time to get the right results.

5   Use what is in your cupboard and fridge and don't get hung up on recipes that call for ingredients you don't have. Swaps are always possible, as long as you think about what the particular ingredient adds to the recipe. Vinegars provide acidity and can be interchangeable or swapped for the sharpness of citrus, while maple syrup may add sweetness but could be swapped with brown sugar. Understand what your ingredients are doing in a recipe and adapt accordingly.

6   Inject flavour into the most basic of kitchen ingredients. Torch those tortillas over an open flame, toast nuts and seeds before use or roast garlic or onions before using in soups and stews. Little adjustments to some key ingredients within a recipe can completely transform them and are well worth taking the time to do.

GARNISH

I'm all for finishing touches, as they can go a long way to amplifying the flavour in a dish. Use the following generously and often!

SEA SALT

FRESHLY GROUND BLACK PEPPER

CHILLI FLAKES

LEMON JUICE

FRESH HERBS

REALLY GOOD EXTRA VIRGIN OLIVE OIL

SERVE

Invest in bowls and plates you want to eat from.
I'm a big believer that food looks better on nice plates –
choose what you like and don't save them for a special
occasion, they should be an integral part of your food.

LEFTOVERS

Please, please don't throw away leftovers. They are often the bones of your next lunch or dinner and there are plenty of ways to inject new life into them. Here are some quick-fix leftover ideas:

Everything tacos
Torched tortillas are perfect for wrapping up leftover meat and veggies with a splodge of hot sauce, a dollop of crème fraîche, lime juice and some herbs.

Leftover salad bowls
Use your favourite fancy bowl and build a bowl of leftovers bulked up with grains and salad leaves, perhaps with a soft-boiled egg and a sharp vinaigrette.

Back of the fridge fried rice
Breathe life into those leftovers by frying with cooked rice and egg and plenty of seasoning.

①
15/30 MINUTE MEALS

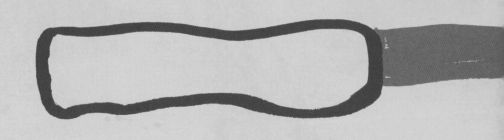

Quick-fix Saucy Pantry Chicken

◎ Serves 4

🕐 10 minutes

🍲 15 minutes

Recipes that rely on elements that can easily be found in your cupboards are always winners in my book; this quick pan-fried chicken recipe is made all the more delicious by using staples like mustard, honey and capers for a punchy sauce. Serve with rice, couscous or just lightly dressed salad leaves.

1 tbsp olive oil
8 rashers of smoked streaky
  bacon, roughly chopped
8 skinless chicken thigh fillets
30g (1oz) butter
4 garlic cloves, thinly sliced
150ml (scant ⅔ cup) white wine
2 tsp Dijon mustard
2 tsp honey
2 tbsp capers
5 dashes of hot sauce, or to taste
Handful of flat-leaf parsley
250g (9oz) tenderstem broccoli
Sea salt and freshly ground
  black pepper

1 Heat the oil in a sauté pan (skillet) and fry the bacon until golden and crisp. Scoop out with a slotted spoon, leaving the fat in the pan. Season the chicken with salt and pepper and fry in the same pan over a medium-high heat for 3–4 minutes on each side until just cooked through.

2 Return the bacon to the pan and add the butter and garlic. Cook for a minute then, once the butter has melted, add the wine, mustard, honey, capers, hot sauce and half of the parsley and let it reduce to a thickened sauce, about 2–3 minutes. Season with salt and pepper.

3 Meanwhile, blanch the tenderstem in boiling water for 2–3 minutes, drain.

4 Serve the chicken with the broccoli, scattered with the remaining parsley.

Griddled Steak with Green Chilli Coriander Sauce

◎ Serves 4

🍶 10 minutes, plus marinating

🍲 10 minutes

A great veggie-packed speedy supper; if you yearn for some extra carbs try serving with roasted sweet potato wedges or some simple boiled new potatoes tossed in melted butter and herbs.

2 × 450g (1lb) sirloin or rump steaks
2 tbsp olive oil, plus extra for brushing
2 garlic cloves, bashed
2 courgettes (zucchini), quite thickly sliced on the diagonal
Bunch of asparagus, trimmed
1 baby gem lettuce, cut into wedges lengthwise
Bunch of spring onions (scallions), trimmed
Sea salt and freshly ground black pepper

For the sauce

100g (3½oz) fresh coriander (cilantro), with roots if you can find them
1 garlic clove
1 small green chilli
Juice of ½ lemon
4–5 tbsp extra virgin olive oil

1   Put the steak in a dish and add the oil, bashed garlic and lots of black pepper and marinate for 30 minutes while you prep your veg.

2   Make your sauce: blitz the coriander (save a handful of leaves to garnish) in a food processor with the garlic, chilli, lemon juice, extra virgin olive oil and a small splash of cold water to loosen. Set aside.

3   Place a large griddle pan over a high heat. Brush your veggies in a little olive oil and char in batches on the hot griddle until tender and a little charred. Set aside on a warm serving platter.

4   Season the steak with salt and sear for 2–3 minutes each side, for medium rare. Cook for another minute if you like your steak more well done. Set aside to rest for a good few minutes then slice thickly and arrange on top of your veggies. Drizzle with the dressing and serve scattered with coriander leaves.

Cheat's Spring Risotto with Orzo, Mint & Courgette

◎ Serves 4–6

🍶 5 minutes

🍲 20 minutes

ⓥᴱ Vegetarian

Orzo is an often overlooked pasta but it's great to stir through soups and stews to add bulk and a silky starchy finish. It's also ideal for a cheat's risotto as it requires a good deal less cooking time than arborio rice and not half as much stirring as for a traditional risotto. Get the basics of this recipe down and you can transform with whatever seasonal vegetables or flavours you fancy.

2 tbsp olive oil
25g (1oz) unsalted butter
1 small onion, finely chopped
2 sprigs of lemon thyme, leaves stripped
350g (12oz) orzo pasta
750ml (3 cups) hot vegetable or chicken stock
2 large courgettes (zucchini), coarsely grated
100g (3½oz) frozen peas
Finely grated zest of 1 lemon, plus a squeeze of juice
125ml (½ cup) double (heavy) cream
1 tbsp finely chopped mint leaves
65g (2½oz) pecorino (or vegetarian alternative), grated
50g (1¾oz) baby spinach leaves
Sea salt and freshly ground black pepper
Extra virgin olive oil, for drizzling

1 Heat the oil and butter in a sauté pan (skillet) and gently fry the onion for 5 minutes before adding the lemon thyme leaves and orzo. Stir together, then add 600ml (2½ cups) of the stock and the courgette. Season well, then cover and cook for 8–10 minutes, stirring occasionally.

2 Add the peas, lemon zest, the rest of the stock and the cream and cook for a further 2–3 minutes. Fold in the mint, pecorino and baby spinach and cook until the spinach has gently wilted.

3 Serve with a squeeze of lemon juice, a good drizzle of extra virgin olive oil and lots of cracked black pepper.

Chicken Piccata

◎ Serves 4

🍶 10 minutes

🍲 15 minutes

A really simple Italian way with chicken that uses butter, white wine, lemon juice and capers to create a wonderfully rich and sharp sauce. Here it's made into a full meal with green beans, spinach and al dente linguine.

1   Place the chicken between two sheets of baking parchment and bash gently with a rolling pin to flatten out until they are between ½–1cm (¼–½in) thick.

2   Cook the pasta in boiling salted water for 10–12 minutes until al dente, drain and return to the pan with 1–2 tablespoons of the cooking water. Blanch the green beans in boiling water for 2 minutes, then drain and cool under cold water.

3   Meanwhile, mix the flour and Parmesan in a dish and season generously with salt and pepper.

4   Put the oil and about two-thirds of the butter in a large frying pan (skillet) and place over a medium-high heat until the butter is foaming. Dredge the chicken breasts in the seasoned flour on all sides, add to the pan, in batches if necessary, and fry for 3–4 minutes each side, or until golden brown and cooked through. Transfer to a plate and keep warm while you finish the dish.

5   With the pan still over a medium heat, pour in the white wine, lemon juice and capers and bring to a steady simmer. Continue to bubble away for a couple of minutes until reduced by half, then whisk in the last of the butter.

6   Add the beans and spinach to the pan and allow the spinach to wilt and the beans to warm through, then add the pasta and toss well. Serve the chicken, pasta and sauce with a good sprinkle of parsley.

4 free-range chicken breasts
400g (14oz) linguini
200g (7oz) green beans
4 tbsp plain (all-purpose) flour
4 tbsp Parmesan cheese, grated
2 tbsp olive oil
100g (3½oz) unsalted butter
200ml (generous ¾ cup) white wine
Juice of ½ lemon
2 tbsp capers
2 handfuls of baby leaf spinach
Sea salt and freshly ground black pepper
Small handful of finely chopped flat-leaf parsley, to serve

My Mum's Spicy Chicken Pittas

◎ Serves 4

▢ 10 minutes, plus marinating

▭ 5–8 minutes

This is such a simple way to cook chicken breasts – the sticky mustard chicken makes use of staple kitchen cupboard ingredients and can be used to stuff hot pitta pockets or to top dressed salad leaves with chickpeas, cherry tomatoes, thinly sliced red onion and a punchy balsamic vinaigrette.

1 tbsp olive oil
1 tbsp wholegrain mustard
2 tsp balsamic vinegar
1 tbsp runny honey
Few dashes of Tabasco
500g (1lb 2oz) free-range chicken breasts, cut into strips
4 wholegrain pitta breads (or 8 mini pittas)
Sea salt and freshly ground black pepper

For the salad

3 large carrots
1 fat baby gem lettuce, leaves shredded
1 tsp toasted fennel seeds
2 tbsp extra virgin olive oil
Good squeeze of lemon juice
2 tbsp mayonnaise
2 tbsp Greek yoghurt

1   Whisk together the olive oil, mustard, vinegar, honey and Tabasco in a shallow dish and add the chicken. Season well and leave to marinate for 30 minutes or so if you can.

2   Prepare the salad: coarsely grate the carrots and toss with the rest of the ingredients. Season to taste and set aside.

3   Place a large pan over a high heat and add the chicken and its marinade. Fry, without moving, for a good few minutes before turning over, allowing it to become lovely and sticky.

4   Lightly toast and split the pittas. Pile the salad and chicken into the pittas and serve.

Lettuce-wrapped Smashburgers with Shredded Pickle Salad

◎ Serves 4

🥄 20 minutes

🍲 10 minutes

Smashburgers were a big deal when we were living in LA: beef mince is pressed down hard on a hot griddle until the edges char and go crisp, while the meat stays nice and tender. You want beef with a good amount of fat in it – although you can always add some diced pancetta or streaky bacon to give the beef a boost in fat and flavour.

500g (1lb 2oz) minced (ground) beef (20% fat)
1 tbsp olive oil
4 slices of American cheese (optional)
4 large sturdy lettuce leaves, such as batavia or iceberg, or for a twist try using large radicchio leaves

For the pickle salad

2 large carrots, shredded
1 cucumber, peeled, deseeded and cut into half-moons
75ml (⅓ cup) distilled malt vinegar
1 tbsp caster (superfine) sugar
1 tsp coriander seeds

For the smashed avo

2 avocados
Handful of cherry tomatoes, finely chopped
1 small green finger chilli, finely chopped (optional)
150g (5oz) Greek yoghurt
2 tbsp extra virgin olive oil
Squeeze of lemon juice
Sea salt and freshly ground black pepper

1 First make your toppings. Mix the carrot and cucumber in a bowl. Put the vinegar, sugar and coriander seeds in a small pan and bring to the boil, then pour over the veggies and set aside.

2 Roughly mash your avocado and stir in the tomatoes, chilli (if using), yoghurt and extra virgin olive oil. Season to taste and add a squeeze of lemon juice.

3 Season the mince and divide into 8 portions (but don't shape them into patties) Heat the oil in a heavy-based frying pan (skillet) over a medium-high until very hot. Place the mince onto the hot pan and press down hard with a spatula.

4 Cook for 3–4 minutes, flip and cook for another 3 minutes until just cooked through. Do not move or flip the patties multiple times, or you won't get a lovely crust and colour on your burgers. Top with the cheese (if using), then add a little splash of water to the pan, cover with a lid and cook for another minute until the cheese has melted. You may need to do this in batches if your pan isn't big enough.

5 Wrap each burger in a lettuce leaf, allowing two patties per burger, add your toppings and devour.

Thai BBQ Fighting Chicken with Crunchy Salad

 Serves 4

🍶 10 minutes, plus marinating

🍲 15 minutes

Ideally you want to cook this fabulous street-food recipe on a barbecue but if it's raining or you don't have one then you can do this on the griddle as in this recipe.

2 lemongrass stalks, peeled
  and chopped
3 garlic cloves
1 red chilli
Large bunch of coriander (cilantro)
3 tbsp soy sauce
2 tbsp brown sugar
2 tbsp rice vinegar
1 tbsp fish sauce
2 tbsp groundnut (peanut) oil
8 free-range chicken thighs (bone
  in and skin on)
Sea salt and white pepper

For the salad

100g (3½oz) kale, shredded
200g (7oz) carrot, grated
¼ red cabbage, shredded
5 spring onions (scallions),
  thinly sliced
2 tbsp smooth peanut butter
1 tbsp rice vinegar
2 tbsp soy sauce
1 tbsp honey
2cm (¾in) piece of fresh ginger
Juice of 1 lime
2 tsp sesame oil

To serve

Handful of coriander (cilantro)
  leaves
Handful of basil leaves
Handful of peanuts, chopped

1   In a pestle and mortar or in a small food processor, mash together the lemongrass, garlic, chilli and coriander stems and roots. Blend with the soy sauce, sugar, rice vinegar and fish sauce, then add the oil and season with sea salt and white pepper. Tip into a shallow bowl, add the chicken thighs and leave to marinate for at least an hour, or overnight.

2   Preheat the oven to 200°C/180°C fan/400°F/Gas 6.

3   Mix all the vegetables for the salad together in a large bowl. Blend the rest of the salad ingredients together to make a dressing, pour over the vegetables and toss well.

4   Place an ovenproof griddle pan over a high heat. Add the chicken thighs and char for a few minutes on each side, then transfer to the oven for 5–6 minutes until tender and cooked through. Serve the chicken with the crunchy salad, a sprinkling of coriander, basil and some peanuts.

Prawn & Basil Stir Fry

◎ Serves 4

🗋 10 minutes, plus
marinating

⎕ 10 minutes

A really simple recipe for pan-fried prawns to get maximum flavour using kitchen cupboard ingredients. Serve this with regular cooked basmati rice or the vibrant raw cauliflower rice here.

2 red Thai chillies
2 garlic cloves
1 tbsp caster (superfine) sugar
1 tbsp fish sauce
2 tbsp soy sauce
2 tbsp sesame oil
16–20 large raw prawns (jumbo shrimp), peeled but tails left on
Large handful of basil leaves
1 tbsp olive oil

For the cauliflower rice

1 large cauliflower
1 tbsp fish sauce
1 tbsp rice vinegar
Juice of 1 lime
2 tsp sesame oil
1 red chilli, deseeded and finely chopped
Good pinch of caster (superfine) sugar
Large handful of coriander (cilantro) leaves

1   In a pestle and mortar or small food processor, blitz the chillies, garlic and sugar. Stir in the fish sauce, soy sauce and 1 tablespoon of sesame oil then pour this over the prawns and leave to marinate for 30 minutes.

2   Coarsely grate the cauliflower and put into a bowl. Mix the fish sauce, rice vinegar, lime juice, sesame oil, chilli and sugar together and stir into the cauliflower. Add the coriander and set aside.

3   Heat a little olive oil in a pan over a high heat. Remove the prawns from the marinade (keep the marinade) and fry, turning once, until they are pink all over. Pour the marinade over the prawns and bubble until it becomes sticky. Add the basil leaves and toss to wilt them in the pan.

4   Serve the sticky prawns with the cauliflower rice.

Creamy Brussels Sprouts Pasta

◎ Serves 4

🫙 10 minutes

🍲 15 minutes

Sprouts are most definitely not just for Christmas. Shot through a food processor, they make a wonderful fresh slaw or, as in this recipe, a great addition to a creamy pasta dish sprinkled with crispy breadcrumbs. Chopped rosemary or thyme is a delicious addition to the pangratatto if you have some.

400g (14oz) orecchiette
1 tbsp olive oil
200g (7oz) diced pancetta
200g (7oz) Brussels sprouts, quartered
3 tbsp crème fraîche
20g (¾oz) Parmesan cheese, grated
1 tbsp finely chopped dill

For the pangrattato

2 tbsp olive oil
Knob of butter
1 garlic clove, thinly sliced
100g (3½oz) fresh white breadcrumbs
Finely grated zest of ½ lemon
Sea salt and freshly ground black pepper

1 Cook the pasta in plenty of boiling salted water for 12–13 minutes until just tender. Drain, reserving 100ml (scant ½ cup) of cooking water.

2 Meanwhile, make the pangrattato. Heat the oil and butter in a large frying pan (skillet) and fry the garlic with the breadcrumbs and lemon zest until golden. Season and set aside.

3 Heat the olive oil in the same pan and gently fry the pancetta until golden, then scoop out with a slotted spoon and set aside. Add the sprouts to the pan and fry, with a splash of water, until they are just tender.

4 Return the crispy pancetta to the pan along with the drained pasta, crème fraîche, Parmesan and reserved cooking water. Stir together with half the dill and check the seasoning. Serve with the pangrattato and the rest of the dill to scatter over.

15/30 Minute Meals

Steak Noodle Bowl with Soy Dressing

◎ Serves 2

⬜ 10 minutes

⬜ 10 minutes

This noodle bowl is easy to adapt using whatever vegetables you have to hand. It's broken down into pan-fried meat (you could also use chicken breast), just-cooked noodles and fresh shredded vegetables and a simple but aromatic dressing.

1   Cook the udon noodles according to the packet instructions, then cool under lukewarm running water and set aside.

2   Place a frying pan (skillet) over a medium-high heat. Rub the steak with the sesame oil and season generously with sea salt and fry for 3–4 minutes on each side until medium rare. Cook for a minute or two longer if you like your steak more well done. Remove from the pan and allow to rest for 5 minutes.

3   Mix together the ingredients for the dressing and pour over the cabbage, radishes, carrot and spring onions in a large bowl. Toss with the noodles and most of the herbs and arrange into two bowls.

4   Slice the steak thinly and arrange on top of the noodles and vegetables. Scatter over the peanuts and the rest of the herbs.

250g (9oz) udon noodles
250g (9oz) rib-eye steak,
   fat trimmed
1 tbsp sesame oil
¼ head of Chinese cabbage,
   thinly sliced
100g (3½oz) radishes, thinly sliced
1 carrot, shredded
4 spring onions (scallions), thinly
   sliced
Good handful of coriander
   (cilantro) leaves
Small handful of mint leaves
Good handful of roughly chopped
   roasted salted peanuts
Sea salt

For the dressing

3 tbsp dark soy sauce
1 tbsp rice wine vinegar
2 tsp caster (superfine) sugar
2cm (¾in) piece of fresh ginger,
   peeled and grated
1 tbsp sesame oil

Crispy Hoisin Duck Lettuce Wraps

◎ Serves 4

⏱ 15 minutes

⏲ 30 minutes

The skin of the duck once crisped is really tasty and adds so much texture and flavour to these lettuce cups. If you lightly bash the toasted sesame seeds before scattering them over it'll release even more of their flavour.

4 confit duck legs

5cm (2in) piece of fresh ginger, finely grated

3 garlic cloves, crushed

2 tbsp honey

2 tbsp dark soy sauce

3 tbsp light soy sauce

2 tbsp hoisin sauce, plus extra to serve

1 tsp Chinese five-spice

2 heads of baby gem lettuce

½ cucumber, peeled, deseeded and sliced into thin batons

1 small carrot, sliced into strips

4 spring onions (scallions), thinly sliced and dropped into iced water

1 red chilli, thinly sliced

Small handful of coriander (cilantro) leaves

1 tbsp toasted sesame seeds

1   Preheat the oven to 220°C/200°C fan/425°F/Gas 7. Place the duck legs on a roasting tray and bake in the oven for 25 minutes.

2   When the duck is almost finished place a large frying pan (skillet) over a medium heat. Add 2 tablespoons of oil from the roasting tray to the frying pan along with the ginger and garlic. Sauté for 2–3 minutes until softened. Add the honey, soy sauces, hoisin sauce and Chinese five-spice to the pan and stir to combine.

3   Pull the duck meat and crispy skin from the bones and shred, discarding any bones. Toss the meat into the sauce in the pan to coat.

4   Separate the baby gem leaves and lay on a platter. Top with the duck, cucumber, carrot, spring onions, chilli, coriander and sesame seeds. Serve with extra dollops of hoisin sauce as needed.

Brown Butter White Fish
with Potatoes & Greens

◎ Serves 4

🥫 10 minutes

🍲 40 minutes

The classic combination of fish doused in nutty brown butter spiked with acidity from lemon juice or vinegar and salty capers is out of this world. It takes little time in the oven but really the whole recipe is minimal effort. You'll also want to revisit the salt-crusted potatoes method shown here time and again.

800g (1lb 12oz) baby potatoes
120g (4oz) fine sea salt
1kg (2lb 4oz) piece of monkfish
  or other firm white fish, skin on
300g (10oz) cherry tomatoes
3 garlic cloves, bashed
60g (2¼oz) butter
1 tbsp olive oil
300g (10oz) leafy greens,
  shredded
Juice of ½ lemon
2 tbsp capers
2 tsp white wine vinegar
40g (1½oz) toasted almond flakes
Sea salt and freshly ground
  black pepper

1   Preheat the oven to 200°C/180°C fan/400°F/Gas 6.

2   Put the potatoes into a large pan with the salt and cover with water. Bring to the boil then simmer gently, uncovered, stirring occasionally until the potatoes are cooked and covered in a thin layer of salt and all the water has evaporated, taking about 30–35 minutes.

3   Meanwhile, put the fish into an ovenproof dish and scatter the tomatoes and garlic around it. Dot with the butter, drizzle with the olive oil and season well. Roast in the oven for 20–25 minutes until the fish is just cooked.

4   Wilt the greens in a covered pan with a little water over a high heat until tender, then drain off any remaining water.

5   Tilt the fish dish to let the buttery juices puddle in a corner, then whisk in the lemon juice, capers and vinegar. Scatter with the flaked almonds and serve with the potatoes and greens.

Creamy Coconut & Lemongrass Fish Stew

◎ Serves 4

🍶 10 minutes

🍲 15 minutes

A really reliable fish curry/stew that is the business on a wet, cold wintery evening. The flavour of this dish relies on that classic Thai flavour combo of salty, sweet and sour so ensure you taste it while it cooks and use fish sauce, sugar and lime juice to find the perfect balance.

4 lemongrass stalks, finely chopped
2 long red chillies, deseeded and finely chopped
4 garlic cloves, crushed
1 tbsp groundnut (peanut) or sunflower oil
1 tbsp medium curry powder
200g (7oz) green beans
400ml (1¾ cups) tin coconut milk
200ml (generous ¾ cup) vegetable stock
500g (1lb 2oz) firm white fish, cut into chunks
1 tbsp soft light brown sugar
1 tbsp Thai fish sauce
2 large handfuls of baby spinach
Juice of 1 lime
Small handful of mint, Thai basil and coriander (cilantro) leaves, to garnish

For the rice

250g (9oz) Thai jasmine long grain rice, rinsed 2–3 times
Pinch of salt

1   Tip the washed rice into a large pan and pour over 500ml (2 cups) cold water and a pinch of salt. Bring to the boil and stir through to prevent the rice from sticking to the bottom. Lower the heat to a simmer and cook for 10 minutes. Remove from the heat and stand for 5 minutes, then fluff up the rice with a fork.

2   While the rice cooks make the curry. Bash the lemongrass, chillies and garlic in a pestle and mortar to form a rough paste (or you can blitz in a mini food processor).

3   Heat the oil in a wok or a large non-stick frying pan (skillet) over a high heat. Add the lemongrass mixture and stir-fry for a minute until fragrant. Add the curry powder and stir-fry until aromatic. Add the beans then pour over the coconut milk and stock. Add the fish then stir in the sugar and fish sauce and cook for 3–4 minutes until the fish is translucent and cooked through.

4   Remove from the heat and add the spinach, lime juice and half the herbs; allow to wilt in the residual heat. Serve with the rice and scatter with the remaining herbs.

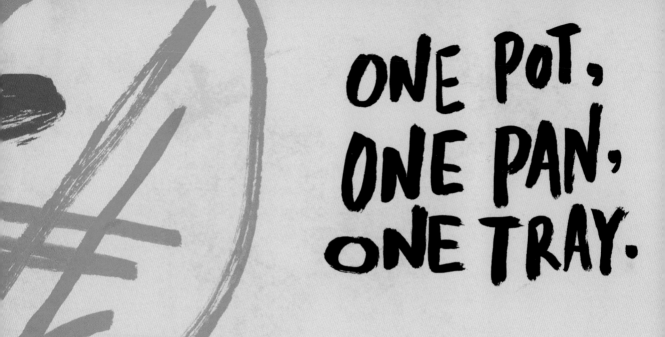

ONE POT, ONE PAN, ONE TRAY.

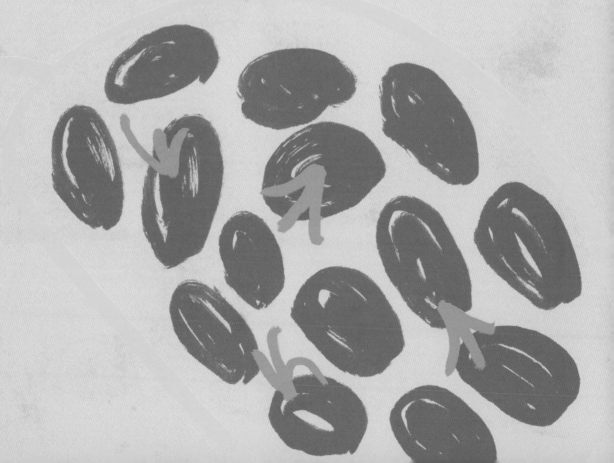

Migas Tacos

◎ Serves 4

🕐 5 minutes

🍲 25 minutes

Ⓥ Vegetarian

Typically a Mexican or Tex-Mex breakfast dish, this also makes a cracking supper. Feel free to experiment with what you add to your eggs: chorizo, black beans or pickled jalapeños go down a treat.

4 large flour tortillas
2 tbsp olive oil
1 small onion, sliced
2 garlic cloves, sliced
2 tbsp chipotle chilli paste
350g (12oz) cherry tomatoes
 or vine tomatoes
2 large handfuls of corn tortilla
 chips, roughly crushed
8 medium free-range eggs, beaten
75g Cheddar cheese (or
 vegetarian alternative), grated
Sea salt and freshly ground
 black pepper

Ideas for toppings

Sliced avocado
Soured cream
Coriander (cilantro) leaves
Lime juice

1   Wrap the flour tortillas in foil and warm in a low oven while you make the migas.

2   Heat the oil in a large non-stick frying pan (skillet) over a medium-high heat. Add the onion and gently fry for 10 minutes until softened. Add the garlic and the chipotle paste and cook for 30 seconds, then stir in the tomatoes and season well.

3   Cook for 10 minutes until the tomatoes have softened down slightly, then stir in the tortilla chips and cook for a minute or two more until they absorb some of the juices but are still a bit crunchy.

4   Season the beaten egg and then pour into the pan, stirring and folding gently, until it scrambles to velvety folds.

5   Scatter each of the warm tortillas with grated Cheddar, then top with the scrambled egg mix, the tomatoes and any toppings you like.

Spiced Yoghurt Roasted Chicken Thighs with Roasted Squash

◎ Serves 4

🕐 10 minutes, plus marinating

🍲 40–45 minutes

Marinating the chicken in yoghurt is worth the wait and results in really tender chicken thighs, here infused with spices like cumin, turmeric and cardamom. Swap the butternut squash with sweet potato or aubergine (eggplant) if you like.

200g (7oz) Greek yoghurt
2 garlic cloves, crushed
3 cardamom pods, crushed
½ tsp ground cinnamon
2 tsp ground cumin
1 tsp ground turmeric
Zest of 1 lemon, plus a squeeze of juice
2 tsp honey
8 free-range chicken thighs (bone in and skin on)
1kg (2lb 4oz) butternut squash, deseeded and cut into wedges
2 red onions, cut into wedges
2 tbsp olive oil
400g (14oz) tin chickpeas, drained and rinsed
Handful of fresh coriander (cilantro), chopped
Sea salt and freshly ground black pepper

1   Preheat the oven to 200°C/180°C fan/400°F/Gas 6.

2   In a bowl mix the yoghurt with the garlic, spices, lemon zest and juice, honey and plenty of seasoning. Add the chicken and marinate for 30 minutes, if you have time.

3   Toss the squash and onions with the oil and tip into a roasting tray. Season well then add the chicken pieces and nestle them into the tray.

4   Roast for 30–35 minutes, turning the squash and onions halfway through, then add the chickpeas and return to the oven for 10 minutes more. Scatter with the coriander and serve.

One Pot, One Pan, One Tray

No Rise, No Fuss One-pan Pizza

◎ Makes 4

🍶 20 minutes

🍲 40 minutes

(VE) Vegetarian

I am well aware that this is NOT traditional pizza but it requires zero rise time and you most likely have the ingredients for the dough in your cupboard. Par-cooking the base in a frying pan guarantees a crisp base. For added texture, sprinkle the pan with polenta or semolina before laying the dough on top. If possible have two or three frying pans on the go, working on the next pizza as one is in the oven.

1 Preheat the oven as high as it will go while you make the sauce. Heat the oil for the sauce in a small pan over a low-medium heat. Add the garlic and cook for a few seconds, then pour in the passata. Season well, then simmer until reduced a little to a lovely thick spreadable sauce. Set aside.

2 Make the dough. Mix the flour, baking powder and salt in a large bowl. Add the water, yoghurt and extra virgin olive oil and mix together and knead until you have a smooth dough.

3 Place a large (25–30cm/10–12in)) heavy-based ovenproof frying pan (skillet) – cast iron is ideal – over a high heat.

4 Divide the dough into four and roll each out to the size of your skillet. Drizzle the pan with a tiny bit of oil and immediately put in one of the pizza bases and cook for a minute until it bubbles lightly, then spread with a quarter of the sauce. Scatter with a quarter of the grated mozzarella and torn buffalo mozzarella. Arrange a quarter of the mushrooms, courgette and artichoke hearts over the pizza.

5 Put into the oven for 8–10 minutes until golden and melted. As soon as it comes out, scatter with rocket leaves and Parmesan and a good drizzle of extra virgin olive oil. Slide onto a board and repeat with the rest of the dough and toppings, devouring the first one as the second cooks.

500g (4 cups) 00 flour
1 tsp baking powder
1 tsp salt
150–200ml (scant ⅔–generous ⅔ cup) warm water
2 tbsp natural yoghurt
2 tbsp extra virgin olive oil
Olive oil, for drizzling

For the sauce

2 tbsp extra virgin olive oil
1 garlic clove, thinly sliced
200ml (generous ¾ cup) passata
Sea salt and freshly ground black pepper

For the toppings

250g (9oz) mozzarella, grated
125g (4oz) ball buffalo mozzarella
125g (4oz) king oyster mushrooms (or other meaty mushroom), thinly sliced and tossed in 1 tbsp olive oil and a pinch of sea salt
1 courgette (zucchini), cut into ribbons with a potato peeler
125g (4oz) jarred artichoke hearts in oil, drained
70g (2½oz) wild rocket (arugula) leaves
Parmesan cheese shavings (or vegetarian alternative)
Extra virgin olive oil

Bengt's Fiskgryta

◎ Serves 4

🍶 15 minutes

🍲 35 minutes

My Swedish father-in-law Bengt makes a seriously good fish stew. His slightly simpler version leaves out the tomatoes and saffron but they are a welcome addition to this creamy fish stew for both colour and richness. Use a good-quality dry white wine that you enjoy drinking and pour yourself a glass while you make this.

20g (¾oz) unsalted butter
2 tbsp olive oil
1 large onion, thinly sliced
1 fennel bulb, thinly sliced
Good pinch of saffron strands
300ml (1¼ cups) hot fresh shellfish
  or fish stock
2 vine tomatoes, chopped
1 tbsp tomato purée (paste)
200ml (generous ¾ cup) white wine
300g (10oz) new potatoes, halved
400g (14oz) salmon, cut into cubes
200g (7oz) large raw prawns
  (jumbo shrimp)
75ml (⅓ cup) double (heavy) cream
Sea salt and freshly ground
  black pepper
1 tbsp chopped dill and crusty
  bread, to serve

1 Melt the butter and oil in a large pan and gently fry the onion and fennel for 10–15 minutes until really lovely and soft. Mix the saffron with the hot stock and set aside.

2 Add the tomatoes and tomato purée to the onions and then splash in the wine and cook for a minute or two before pouring in the saffron stock. Add the new potatoes, season with salt and pepper and simmer for 15 minutes until the potatoes are just tender.

3 Add the salmon and prawns and cook for 4–5 minutes until both are cooked, then stir in the cream. Serve with a scattering of dill and some crusty bread.

Chicken & Ginger Rice Congee

◎ Serves 6

🍶 10 minutes, plus soaking

🍲 1¼ hours

A classic breakfast dish in many parts of Asia, this savoury rice porridge is rich and comforting. Use chicken on the bone to add extra flavour. While we lived in Los Angeles, I would take my son Noah to eat this most Sunday mornings at a hole-in-the-wall Thai breakfast joint – it brings back great memories.

225g (8oz) short grain rice
1.4 litres (6 cups) water
4 free-range chicken legs
  (bone in and skin on)
3cm (1¼in) piece of fresh ginger,
  peeled and shredded
200g (7oz) greens (spring greens,
  kale, cavolo nero or Chinese
  cabbage), shredded
Sea salt

Topping options

Shop-bought pickled vegetables
  (ginger, daikon, cucumber, carrot)
Roughly chopped roasted peanuts
Bunch of spring onions (scallions),
  thinly sliced
Bunch of coriander (cilantro),
  leaves picked and roughly
  chopped
Chilli oil or peanut chilli paste,
  for drizzling
Soy sauce, for drizzling

1   Wash the rice well and soak for 30 minutes. Drain and put into a large pan with the water and a good pinch of salt. Bring to the boil, then add the chicken legs and ginger. Return to the boil, then partially cover with a lid, reduce to a very gentle simmer and cook for 1 hour until the rice is cooked but a bit soupy. Stir every so often and add a little more water if it starts to look a bit thick. Add the greens for the last 10 minutes of cooking time.

2   Remove the chicken from the pan and shred the meat, discarding the skin and bones, then return to the congee in the pan.

3   Serve in deep bowls with a selection of toppings to scatter and drizzle over.

One Pot, One Pan, One Tray

Griddled Chicken, Basil & Sweetcorn Fajitas

◎ Serves 4

⌀ 10 minutes

⬓ 10 minutes

A quick-fix chicken dinner that is easy to assemble. Heat the tortillas directly over a gas ring with tongs or on a hot griddle pan to get the best from them. If you have some nice ripe avocados, a dollop of creamy guacamole would work brilliantly to top these wraps.

1 Mix the chicken strips with the sliced onion, chipotle paste and half the lime juice. Season well.

2 Place a large frying pan (skillet) over a high heat with a little oil. Add the chicken and onion mix and fry until the chicken is cooked all the way through. Don't be tempted to move the contents of the pan too much, allow it to slightly catch and char before stirring.

3 Add the sweetcorn to the pan with the butter and cook for 2–3 minutes until tender. Fold through the basil.

4 Divide the contents of the pan between the warmed tortillas. Dollop with the soured cream, scatter with the cheese, diced red onion and coriander leaves, sprinkle with cayenne pepper and a squeeze of lime juice to your taste before serving.

4 free-range chicken breasts, sliced into strips
1 red onion, thinly sliced
1 tbsp chipotle chilli paste
Juice of 1 lime
1 tbsp olive oil
250g (9oz) sweetcorn kernels
25g (1oz) butter
Large handful of basil leaves, torn
4 small flour tortillas, warmed
4 tbsp soured cream
40g (1½oz) hard ricotta, grated
1 small red onion, finely diced
Small handful of coriander (cilantro) leaves
Pinch of cayenne pepper
1 lime, halved
Sea salt and freshly ground black pepper

Vietnamese-style Crepe with Pork & Prawns

◎ Serves 4

🕐 10 minutes, plus resting

🍲 20 minutes

This savoury Vietnamese pancake made with prawns and beansprouts is incredibly popular and makes a great light supper with a difference. The key here is to serve it with plenty of fresh elements like lettuce, mint and Thai basil.

100g (scant 1 cup) white rice flour
15g (½oz) cornflour (cornstarch)
1 tsp ground turmeric
½ tsp salt
150ml (5fl oz) cold water
200ml (generous ¾ cup) coconut milk
2 tbsp groundnut (peanut) or mild olive oil
8 spring onions (scallions), finely shredded
250g (9oz) raw king prawns (jumbo shrimp), roughly chopped
300g (10oz) pancetta, finely diced
150g (5oz) beansprouts
Lettuce leaves, coriander (cilantro) leaves, Thai basil and mint leaves, to serve

For the dipping sauce
Juice of 1 lime
1 tbsp fish sauce
3 tbsp soy sauce
1 green finger chilli, finely chopped
1 tbsp palm or brown sugar

1   Whisk the flours with the turmeric and salt, then add the water and coconut milk and mix to a smooth batter. Set aside to rest for 1 hour. Blend the ingredients for the sauce together and set aside.

2   Heat the oil in a roughly 20cm (8in) frying pan (skillet) and fry the spring onions, prawns and pancetta together for 5–6 minutes over a high heat until the prawns are pink and the pancetta starts to become golden. Scoop out of the pan and set aside.

3   Wipe the pan out with kitchen paper so there is just a thin layer of oil all over and place back over quite a high heat. Spread a quarter of the filling and a handful of beansprouts over the base of the pan.

4   Stir the batter well and pour in a quarter of it so it sizzles, swirling the pan to make a thin layer all over the filling. Cover and cook for 2–3 minutes, then uncover and cook for a minute or two more until the edges and underside are golden and crisp. Slide onto a plate and keep warm while you repeat with the remaining filling and batter.

5   Serve the crepes with lettuce leaves and plenty of fresh herbs, and the dipping sauce on the side.

Roast Thai Red Curry Chicken

◎ Serves 6

🖊 10 minutes

🍲 1¼ hours

A wonderful way to mix up the Sunday roast. Replace aubergine (eggplant) with vegetables like sweet potato or squash. Once cooked the rice can be seasoned with fish sauce and a twist of lime juice for even more flavour.

1 large free-range chicken
   (about 1.8kg/4lb)
2 tbsp Thai red curry paste
1 tbsp unsalted butter, softened
2 kaffir lime leaves
1 lemongrass stalk, bashed
1 large aubergine (eggplant),
   cut into chunks
1 whole garlic bulb, cloves
   separated but left unpeeled
2–3 tbsp olive oil
225g (8oz) basmati rice, rinsed
400ml (1¾ cups) tin coconut milk
Handful of coriander (cilantro),
   stalks and leaves chopped
Sea salt and freshly ground
   black pepper

To serve

1 tbsp fish sauce
Juice of ½ lime
Sriracha sauce

1   Preheat the oven to 200°C/180°C fan/400°F/Gas 6.

2   Untruss your chicken and put it into a roasting tray. Mix the curry paste and butter together and spread all over your chicken. Put the lime leaves and lemongrass inside the cavity.

3   Toss the aubergine and garlic with the olive oil, season well, then scatter around the chicken. Roast for 1 hour until the aubergine is really tender and the chicken just cooked.

4   Pour any juices from inside the chicken out into the tray then put the bird and the veg onto a warm serving plate, squeeze the flesh out of the garlic cloves, cover and rest. Increase the oven temperature to 220°C/200°C fan/425°F/Gas 7.

5   Add the rice to the tray and toss well then pour over the coconut milk and season with salt and pepper. Bring to a bubble by placing it over a high heat on the hob, then stir and cover with foil. Return the tray to the oven for 15 minutes until the rice is cooked and has absorbed the coconut milk. Scatter with coriander and season to taste with the fish sauce and lime. Serve with the roast chicken, aubergine and garlic, and some sriracha.

Oven-roasted Ratatouille

◎ Serves 4–6

⌂ 10 minutes

⌂ 1¼ hours

(VE) Vegetarian

A tweak on the classic French ratatouille, which of course is delicious as it is, but with pasta stirred through the roast vegetables it makes a substantial midweek meal. Go the extra mile and serve with burrata or mozzarella balls for a real treat.

2 aubergines (eggplants), cut into 2cm (¾in) cubes
2 courgettes (zucchini), halved lengthways and cut into 1cm (½in) thick pieces
2 red onions, cut into wedges
250g (9oz) cherry tomatoes
2 red (bell) peppers, deseeded and sliced
10 garlic cloves, unpeeled
1 tsp chilli flakes
4 sprigs of fresh oregano, leaves stripped
5 tbsp olive oil
Sea salt and freshly ground black pepper

To serve
350g (12oz) short pasta
Drizzle of aged balsamic vinegar
40g (1½oz) Parmesan cheese (or vegetarian alternative), grated
Handful of fresh basil leaves

1   Preheat the oven to 200°C/180°C fan/400°F/Gas 6.

2   Toss the vegetables in a large roasting tray (or two) with the garlic, chilli flakes and oregano. Season well and toss with the oil, then roast for 1¼ hours, turning every so often, until lovely and tender and broken down into a glorious mush. Once the garlic cloves are roasted, remove their skins, and mash with the back of a fork before returning to the roasting tin.

3   Meanwhile cook the pasta in boiling salted water for 10–12 minutes until tender, then drain, toss through the contents of the roasting tin and serve in deep bowls. Finish with a drizzle of balsamic vinegar and scatter with the Parmesan and basil leaves.

HAVING A KITCHEN THAT IS
WELL ORGANISED IS THE
CORNERSTONE OF GREAT
COOKING.

One-pan Chicken Saltimbocca with Courgettes & Tenderstem

○ Serves 4

◻ 10 minutes

◻ 40 minutes

I am in love with saltimbocca so you will have to excuse me if you've seen various iterations of this recipe previously. It's a simple method that instantly leaves you with tender chicken with a crisp salty exterior. Here it's served with courgette (zucchini), broccoli and potatoes for a straight-to-the-table supper.

1 red onion, thinly sliced

400g (14oz) red-skinned potatoes, thinly sliced

200g (7oz) cherry tomatoes

2 courgettes (zucchini), cut into batons

2 tbsp olive oil, plus extra for drizzling

200g (7oz) tenderstem broccoli

100ml (scant ½ cup) white wine

4 small free-range chicken breasts, butterflied

12 fresh sage leaves

8 slices of prosciutto

Sea salt and freshly ground black pepper

1 Preheat the oven to 200°C/180°C fan/400°F/Gas 6.

2 In a large roasting tray, toss the onion, potatoes, tomatoes and courgette with the oil. Season well and roast for 20 minutes. Add the broccoli and roast for a further 5–6 minutes.

3 Remove the tray from the oven, turn the vegetables and splash in the wine. Place the butterflied chicken breasts on top, scatter with the sage, drizzle with a little more oil and season well.

4 Arrange the prosciutto on top of each chicken breast in a scrumpled fashion and roast for a further 15 minutes until the chicken is tender and cooked and the prosciutto is crispy.

Mee Goreng

◎ Serves 4

🕐 15 minutes

🍲 10 minutes

An Indonesian street food classic that is packed with flavour and zing. You can use any mix of veggies you like: try shredded carrot, Chinese cabbage and red peppers or baby corn, sugar snaps and asparagus, depending on the season. If you can't get hold of kecap manis, substitute with dark soy sauce and 1 heaped teaspoon of dark brown sugar.

2 tbsp vegetable oil

2 garlic cloves, thinly sliced

5 spring onions (scallions), thinly sliced

225g (8oz) firm tofu, cut into 2cm (¾in) pieces

200g (7oz) raw king prawns (jumbo shrimp)

2 pak choi or choi sum, quartered

100g (3½oz) green beans, cut into short pieces

300g (10oz) fresh egg noodles

Large handful of beansprouts

1 red chilli, finely sliced, to serve

Lime wedges, to serve

For the sauce

2 tbsp kecap manis

2 tbsp soy sauce

1 tbsp tomato ketchup

1 tbsp fish sauce

1½ tbsp sambal oelek (or 1 tsp chilli flakes)

1   Blend all the ingredients for the sauce together and set aside.

2   Heat the oil in a wok or non-stick frying pan (skillet) over a high heat. Add the garlic, spring onions and tofu and cook until the tofu is starting to colour. Add the prawns and cook for 2–3 minutes until just pink all over.

3   Add the pak choi and beans and stir-fry for a minute or two, then add the noodles and sauce.

4   Stir and toss together until the noodles are hot and everything is coated in the sticky sauce. Fold through the beansprouts, sprinkle with red chilli and serve straight away with lime wedges to squeeze over.

One Pot, One Pan, One Tray

Chicken Scarpariello

○ Serves: 4

⌂ 20 minutes

⌂ 25 minutes

An American-Italian classic that gets its flavour from the best-quality Italian sausages you can track down. Jars of pickled peppers are often overlooked on supermarket shelves but for a recipe like this they add a sweet and slightly spicy heat and great colour.

1 Preheat the oven to 200°C/180°C fan/400°F/Gas 6.

2 Heat the oil in a large low-sided casserole dish over a high heat. Add the sausages and chicken and cook until brown all over. Remove from the pan and set aside.

3 Add the onion, garlic and red pepper to the pan and cook for 5 minutes until softened. Add the rosemary, white wine and vinegar and bubble for a minute then return the chicken and sausages to the pan. Add the potatoes, stock and pickled peppers. Season well and put into the oven to cook for 20 minutes until the chicken is cooked and the sauce has thickened a little.

4 Serve scattered with parsley.

3 tbsp olive oil

300g (10oz) Italian or herb sausages, thickly sliced

300g (10oz) free-range skinless chicken thigh fillets, cut into 2cm (¾in) pieces

1 red onion, thinly sliced

2 garlic cloves, thinly sliced

1 red (bell) pepper, deseeded and sliced

2 sprigs of rosemary

150ml (scant ⅔ cup) white wine

2 tsp white wine vinegar

300g (10oz) new potatoes, halved

250ml (1 cup) stock

8 pickled peppers, such as peppadew or guindilla

Sea salt and freshly ground black pepper

Handful of chopped flat-leaf parsley, to serve

Steamed Ginger & Spring Onion Fish with Noodles & Broccoli

◎ Serves 4

🗍 10 minutes

🍲 25 minutes

A one-tray roasted fish dish inspired by those wonderful platters of whole steamed fish you see in Chinese restaurants. While this may not have the grand presentation of white tablecloths, chopsticks and plates warmed by tealights, it's ideal for a midweek dinner and is fairly easy to prepare.

250g (9oz) vermicelli rice noodles
300g (10oz) tenderstem broccoli
Bunch of spring onions (scallions), trimmed
1 garlic clove, thinly sliced
3cm (1in) piece of fresh ginger, peeled and cut into matchsticks
1 long red chilli, thinly sliced into rounds
2 tbsp sunflower oil
2 tbsp water
1kg (2lb 4oz) piece (or four 250g/9oz pieces) of firm white fish, such as bream or bass
2 tbsp soy sauce
1 tbsp rice vinegar
2 tsp palm or caster (superfine) sugar
1 tbsp sesame oil
2 tsp toasted sesame seeds
Handful of coriander (cilantro) leaves

1 Preheat the oven to 190°C/170°C fan/375°F/Gas 5.

2 Put the noodles into a large bowl, pour boiling water over them and leave to stand for 10 minutes, then drain.

3 Put the broccoli, spring onions, garlic, ginger and chilli into a roasting tray. Add the oil and water, cover with foil and roast for 10 minutes. Uncover and stir, then top with the fish. Blend the soy sauce, rice vinegar, sugar and sesame oil together and pour over the veggies and fish, then re-cover and return to the oven for a further 10 minutes until the fish is just cooked.

4 Remove the fish from the tray and fold the cooked noodles into all that sauciness until thoroughly coated. Return the fish to the tray, scatter with sesame seeds and coriander leaves and serve.

Saffron Chicken Stew
with Pearl Barley & Savoy Cabbage

◎ Serves 6

🕓 15 minutes

🍲 1¼ hours

A simple, warming chicken stew that's ideal for sick days and those dark and cold winter evenings. It's a reliable bowl of comfort that lets you use up any vegetables that might be unloved in the bottom of the fridge. Feel free to add root vegetables, spinach, peas or whatever else takes your fancy.

2 tbsp olive oil
1 large onion, thinly sliced
2 garlic cloves, finely grated
1 large carrot, finely diced
1 celery stick, finely diced
Pinch of saffron strands
1 smallish free-range chicken
  (1.2–1.4 kg/2lb 10oz–3lb 2oz),
  untrussed
200ml (generous ¾ cup) white wine
1 litre (4 cups) fresh chicken stock
300ml (1¼ cups) water
200g (7oz) pearl barley
1 small savoy cabbage, leaves
  separated and kept whole
Squeeze of lemon juice
Handful of chopped flat-leaf
  parsley
Sea salt and freshly ground
  black pepper

1   Heat the oil in a large casserole and gently fry the onion, garlic, carrot and celery for 10 minutes until softened. Stir in the saffron.

2   Season the chicken well and sit on top of the vegetables. Pour in the wine and bubble for a minute or two before adding the stock, water and a little more seasoning.

3   Pour the pearl barley around the chicken and stir in, then cover and bring to a simmer. Cook very gently for 1 hour until the chicken is very tender and falling apart. Remove the chicken and set aside until cool enough to handle.

4   Shred the meat from the chicken. Add the cabbage leaves to the juicy stock and cook for 3–4 minutes. Return the chicken meat to the pan and warm through then serve in bowls with a squeeze of lemon juice and a scattering of parsley.

Roasted White Fish with Confit Cherry Tomatoes

◎ Serves 4

◌ 10 minutes

◻ 1 hour

Roasting whole white fish like hake or haddock really makes an occasion of it. By roasting cherry tomatoes with aubergine (eggplant), peppers and garlic, you create the perfect juicy sauce to enjoy with the tender fish and it can all be served straight to the table in the roasting tray.

400g (14oz) cherry tomatoes
1 large aubergine (eggplant),
    cut into 2cm (¾in) pieces
2 red (bell) peppers, deseeded
    and thinly sliced
1 whole garlic bulb, cloves
    separated but left unpeeled
170ml (6fl oz) olive oil
6 sprigs of fresh thyme
500g (1lb 2oz) piece of cod (or
    another firm white fish fillet)
1 tbsp extra virgin olive oil
Sea salt and freshly ground
    black pepper

To serve

Crusty bread
Green leaves

1   Preheat the oven to 180°C/160°C fan/350°F/Gas 4. Put the cherry tomatoes, aubergine, peppers and garlic cloves in a roasting tray, toss with the oil and thyme and season well.

2   Roast for 45–50 minutes, turning occasionally, until the vegetables are tender and caramelised.

3   Season the fish and nestle into the roasted veg, then return the tray to the oven and cook for 15–20 minutes until the fish is just cooked. Squeeze the garlic out of the skins before serving with lots of crusty bread to mop up the juices and some green leaves.

My Ultimate Meatballs

◎ Serves 4

⎕ 10 minutes, plus chilling

⏲ 40 minutes

Easily one of my most requested recipes, these meatballs are always a winner. The pancetta and buttermilk provide both flavour and tenderness and if you cook these meatballs in an ovenproof saucepan you can finish them in a hot oven with some freshly torn pieces of mozzarella and basil leaves for truly showstopping results.

4 tbsp olive oil
2 garlic cloves, thinly sliced
700g (1lb 8oz) passata
120ml (½ cup) dry white wine
1 tsp dried oregano
1 tsp dried red chilli flakes

For the meatballs

250g (9oz) good-quality minced (ground) beef
250g (9oz) good-quality minced (ground) pork
100g (3½oz) rashers of pancetta, finely chopped
1 onion, finely chopped
3 garlic cloves, grated
60ml (4 tbsp) buttermilk
50g (2oz) breadcrumbs
1 tbsp dried oregano
Small handful of finely chopped flat-leaf parsley
1 medium free-range egg, lightly beaten
Sea salt and freshly ground black pepper

To serve

Fresh tagliatelle
Parmesan cheese shavings

1   Put all the ingredients for the meatballs into a large bowl. Season with salt and pepper and mix until completely and evenly combined.

2   Shape into large golf ball-sized meatballs by rolling them with wet hands. Transfer to a large baking sheet, cover with cling film and leave in the fridge to firm up for 30 minutes.

3   Place a large frying pan (skillet) over a medium-high heat and add a good glug of the olive oil. Fry the meatballs (in batches if necessary) until browned on all sides, about 8–10 minutes, then transfer to a plate lined with kitchen paper.

4   Add the rest of the oil to the pan, reduce the heat and add the garlic. Slowly fry until just golden but not browned.

5   Increase the heat again and pour in the passata and white wine and stir through. Season with the dried oregano, chilli flakes and salt and pepper. Bring to a steady simmer and allow to cook for 5–6 minutes before returning the meatballs to the pan and gently turning with a tablespoon to coat them in the sauce. Cover the pan with a lid and simmer for 20 minutes.

6   Serve with just cooked fresh tagliatelle and plenty of Parmesan shavings.

PREP IT AHEAD,
COOK IT LATER.

Spatchcock Buffalo Roast Chicken, Sweet Potato Fries & Share Salad

◎ Serves 4

🍶 30 minutes

🍲 45 minutes

I have been churning out this simple recipe for so many years in our house that it has become a firm favourite when it comes to an easy Saturday night treat. Spatchcocking the whole bird is a great way to cook it quickly with the crispiest results. Slathered in a homemade buffalo sauce it's a winner every time.

110g (4oz) unsalted butter
120ml (½ cup) hot chilli sauce
½ tsp smoked sweet paprika
1 tbsp runny honey
1 free-range chicken (about 1.6kg /3lb 8oz)
Sea salt and freshly ground black pepper

For the salad

50g (2oz) blue cheese, crumbled
3 tbsp Greek yoghurt
1 tbsp mayonnaise
1 large apple, peeled and cut into matchsticks
6–7 celery sticks and leaves, thinly sliced
2 romaine lettuces, leaves separated
50g (2oz) toasted walnut pieces
Runny honey, for drizzling

For the fries

700g (1lb 8oz) sweet potatoes, cut into fries
2 tsp cornflour (cornstarch)
2 tbsp olive oil

1   Preheat the oven to 210°C/190°C fan/410°F/Gas 7.

2   Put the butter, hot sauce, paprika, honey and plenty of seasoning into a pan and bring to the boil, then reduce the heat and simmer for 5 minutes until slightly thickened.

3   Meanwhile, place the bird breast-side down on a board and, using a heavy pair of sharp scissors (or poultry shears), cut along either side of the backbone to remove it. Open the bird out and flip it over breast side up and, using your fist, push down hard on the breast to break the bone. Put the flattened chicken into a large roasting tray and brush over half the sauce. Roast in the oven for 40–45 minutes until golden and cooked through.

4   Spread the sweet potato fries on a baking sheet and toss all over with the cornflour to form a thin layer. Drizzle with oil and season with sea salt and roast for 30–40 minutes, turning occasionally, until golden and crisp.

5   Blend the blue cheese, yoghurt and mayonnaise together with a fork until smooth (loosen with a splash of water if you need to), then toss with the apple and celery. Lay the lettuce leaves out on a platter and spoon the apple and celery into them then scatter with toasted walnuts and drizzle with honey.

6   When the chicken is done, remove from the oven and portion into breasts, wings, and legs. Warm the remaining buffalo sauce and drizzle over the top. Serve the chicken with the chips and salad and dig in!

Skehan Family Shepherd's Pie

◎ Serves 4–6

⬠ 20 minutes

⬡ 3–3¼ hours

You can never guess the recipes that will resonate with readers and viewers but this indulgent shepherd's pie was certainly one of them. I cooked it on my television show *Family Food In Minutes* and within a couple of days Ireland had sold out of lamb shanks. If the shanks aren't fork-tender at the end of the cooking time, persevere, add more water and keep simmering until they are.

2 tbsp olive oil
4 lamb shanks
1 large onion, finely chopped
2 medium carrots, finely chopped
3 garlic cloves, thinly sliced
6 sprigs of fresh thyme
500ml (2 cups) fresh chicken stock
2 tbsp tomato purée (paste)
1 tbsp Worcestershire sauce
2 tbsp tomato ketchup
Sea salt and freshly ground
   black pepper

For the mash

1.5kg (3lb 5oz) potatoes, peeled
   and cut into chunks
75g (3oz) butter
100ml (scant ½ cup) double
   (heavy) cream
1 free-range egg yolk
6 spring onions (scallions),
   thinly sliced

1   Heat half the olive oil in a casserole over a medium heat. Season the lamb shanks, add to the casserole and brown all over, then remove and set aside. Add the rest of the oil to the pan and soften the onion and carrots for 5–6 minutes. Add the garlic and thyme sprigs and cook for a minute or two more.

2   Return the lamb shanks to the pan and pour over the stock and stir through the tomato purée and Worcestershire sauce until combined. Season well and bring to the boil, then reduce to a simmer and cook gently, partially covered, for 2½ hours, turning the lamb occasionally, until the lamb shanks are tender and falling apart and the sauce is reduced.

3   Meanwhile make the mash: put the potatoes into a pan of cold salted water, bring to the boil and simmer for 15 minutes until tender. Drain and tip back into the pan and place over a low heat to allow them to steam and dry. Add the butter, cream and egg yolk. Using a potato masher, mash the potatoes until smooth and creamy. Stir in the spring onions and season to taste.

4   Preheat the oven to 180°C/160°C fan/350°F/Gas 4.

5   When the lamb is tender, shred the meat from the bone into the sauce, stir in the ketchup and transfer to an ovenproof baking dish. Top with the champ mash, using a spoon to make a nice pattern. Give the topping an extra sprinkle of freshly ground black pepper and bake in the oven for 25 minutes until the top is starting to brown and the sauce is bubbling up around the edges.

CLEAN AS YOU GO WHILE YOU'RE IN THE ZONE.

Charred Lamb Kebabs with Pickled Onions & Saffron Yoghurt

◎ Serves 4

⏱ 20 minutes, plus marinating

🍲 6–8 minutes

Growing up in Ireland, a summer barbecue usually entailed burnt sausages and burgers snaffled under an umbrella. But something has happened in Ireland more recently where we are embracing our unpredictable weather with year-round sea swimming, outdoor hiking and barbecue afficionados perfecting their grill game, rain or shine. Whatever the weather, these lamb kebabs are at their best cooked over an open flame, giving a smoky flavour and a lightly charred texture.

800g (1lb 12oz) lamb leg, diced into chunks
5 garlic cloves, grated
1 heaped tbsp ras el hanout
2 tbsp olive oil
4 large pitta breads
200g (7oz) hummus
Handful of flat-leaf parsley or coriander (cilantro) leaves
Sea salt and freshly ground black pepper

For the lemon and saffron yoghurt

Small pinch of saffron strands
2 tbsp boiling water
200g (7oz) Greek yoghurt
2 garlic cloves, finely grated
Zest of ½ lemon

For the pickled onions

2 red onions, thinly sliced
1 tbsp coriander seeds
Juice of ½ lemon
Pinch of sugar
1 tbsp extra virgin olive oil

1   Put the lamb into a large bowl with the garlic, ras el hanout and the olive oil. Season with sea salt and toss to combine completely. Leave the lamb to sit, covered with cling film, in the fridge for at least 1 hour. Alternatively make this ahead of time and leave to marinate overnight.

2   While the lamb marinates, prepare the yoghurt sauce: infuse the saffron strands in the hot water in a small bowl and leave to stand for 5 minutes. Add the remaining ingredients and mix well to combine. Season to taste and set aside.

3   To make the pickled onions toss the red onions and coriander seeds with the lemon juice and sugar and season generously with sea salt. Set aside to let the onions soften and pickle.

4   Once the spices have permeated the meat, thread the lamb pieces onto eight metal skewers and arrange on a large baking sheet. Place the lamb skewers to cook over a hot barbecue or a scorching hot griddle pan for 3 minutes on each side, or until medium rare. Turn as needed until you have a lightly charred exterior and a blushing pink interior. While the lamb cooks, toast the pitta breads on the barbecue or just in a toaster.

5   Spread each pitta with hummus, slide the lamb off the skewers and place on top of the pitta with the pickled onion and herbs. Drizzle with the yoghurt sauce before tucking in.

My Ultimate Chicken Curry

◎ Serves 4

🧴 10 minutes, plus marinating

🍲 30 minutes

Curry aficionados will have to excuse this rather slapdash, inauthentic version of a chicken curry but it's the type of recipe that is the workhorse of quick and easy cooking. The core ingredients can be swapped as needed but the sauce and flavour relies on getting your hands on a really good garam masala.

500g (1lb 2oz) free-range skinless chicken thigh fillets, halved or quartered
2 tbsp groundnut (peanut) oil
25g (1oz) unsalted butter
1 heaped tbsp garam masala
300g (10oz) baby new potatoes, quartered lengthways, or diced sweet potato
250ml (1 cup) chicken stock
400g (14oz) tin chopped tomatoes
175g (6oz) pointy cabbage, shredded
100g (3½oz) frozen peas
100ml (scant ½ cup) double (heavy) cream
Handful of fresh coriander (cilantro) leaves
Sea salt and freshly ground black pepper
Steamed rice and naan bread, to serve

For the marinade

1 onion, grated
3 garlic cloves, grated
Large thumb-sized piece of fresh ginger, finely grated
2 tbsp garam masala spice mix
125g (4oz) natural yoghurt

1   Mix all the marinade ingredients together in a large bowl. Add the chicken and plenty of seasoning and allow to marinate for 20 minutes.

2   Heat the oil in a large sauté pan over a medium-high heat. Fry the chicken (in batches if necessary) until golden brown on all sides.

3   Add the butter and the garam masala and allow to coat the chicken then add the potatoes and pour in the stock and tomatoes. Bring to a steady simmer, then turn the heat to low and simmer gently for 15 minutes. Stir through the shredded cabbage, peas and cream, then cover and cook for a further 5 minutes until the cabbage has wilted and the chicken is cooked through and coated in sauce.

4   Scatter over the coriander and serve with steamed rice and naan bread.

Prep it Ahead, Cook it Later

Korean Fried Chicken Bowls

◎ Serves 4

⬦ 15 minutes, plus marinating

⬦ 30 minutes

Super-crispy chicken bathed in a sauce made spicy by the addition of gochujang, Korea's famous spice paste. In this recipe, nuggets of chicken thigh meat are made crispy without a deep-fat fryer and instead are baked in the oven unashamedly with the help of crushed cornflakes. It's a crispy chicken tip that works a treat.

1   Preheat the oven to 200°C/180°C fan/400°F/Gas 6.

2   In a large bowl, mix the buttermilk with a generous season of sea salt and ground black pepper. Add the chicken to the bowl and marinate for at least 30 minutes. Set aside.

3   Pour the cornflakes in a large freezer bag and crush them with a rolling pin to a coarse powder. Add the flour, chilli and garlic powders to the bag along with salt and pepper. Seal the bag and shake the mix until combined.

4   Pour the dry mix into a large wide shallow bowl. One by one using tongs, dip each marinated chicken piece (shaking off any excess) in the dry mix until coated on all sides.

5   Arrange the chicken on a baking sheet with parchment paper and lightly spritz with sunflower oil spray. Cook in the oven for 30 minutes or until the chicken is cooked and crispy, turning halfway through to make sure they're golden on all sides.

6   While the chicken cooks, prepare the sauce. In a small saucepan whisk together the garlic, ginger, soy sauce, gochujang, rice wine vinegar, sesame oil and brown sugar.

7   Place the saucepan over a medium heat and bring to a low simmer, cooking until the sugar is just dissolved – about 3 minutes. Set aside.

8   Once the chicken has cooked, brush with the sauce.

9   Assemble serving bowls with the sticky rice, cabbage, spring onions, radishes, chicken pieces, sesame seeds and plenty of coriander. Drizzle with more of the spicy sauce as needed.

For the chicken
250ml (1 cup) buttermilk
8 free-range chicken thighs (bone in and skin on), cut into bite-sized pieces
100g (3½oz) cornflakes
85g (3oz) plain (all-purpose) flour
2 tsp chilli powder
2 tsp garlic powder
Sunflower oil spray

For the sauce
8 cloves of garlic, finely grated
1 large thumb-sized piece of ginger, finely grated
6 tbsp light soy sauce
70g (2 ½oz) gochujang (Korean chilli paste)
4 tbsp rice wine vinegar
1 tbsp sesame oil
2 tbsp dark brown sugar

For the bowls
250g (9oz) sticky rice, cooked
½ head red cabbage, thinly sliced
6 spring onions (scallions), thinly sliced
Handful of radishes, finely sliced
1 tbsp toasted sesame seeds
A good handful of coriander leaves
Sea salt and freshly ground black pepper

Smoky Chicken Taco Night

◎ Serves 6

🍶 15 minutes

🍲 15 minutes

The beauty of homemade tacos is that when it comes to serving it's a perfect excuse to get everyone to assemble their own. All the different elements can be laid out on the table and from there, it's choose your own taco adventure time! Take the time to char the corn tortillas on a hot griddle pan or over an open flame using tongs – it makes such a difference to their flavour.

2 tbsp olive oil
2 red onions, quartered
750g (1lb 10oz) free-range skinless chicken thigh fillets, sliced
3 garlic cloves, grated
1 tsp ground cumin
1 tbsp chipotle powder

To serve

¼ red cabbage, very finely shredded
Juice of 2 limes, plus wedges to serve
Pinch of sugar
Drizzle of extra virgin olive oil
6 large flour or corn tortillas, warmed
1 red onion, thinly sliced
1 large avocado, sliced
Guacamole
Handful of coriander (cilantro) leaves
Sea salt and freshly ground black pepper

1   Toss the olive oil, red onion, chicken, garlic, cumin and chipotle powder together in a bowl until completely coated. Place a large griddle pan over a high heat until hot, then add the chicken and red onion and allow to char on all sides until the chicken is cooked through and the red onion wedges are tender. Keep warm in a low oven while you prepare the toppings.

2   Toss the shredded red cabbage with the lime juice, a good pinch of sugar and some seasoning. Add a drizzle of extra virgin olive oil and set aside to pickle.

3   Spoon the chicken and onion wedges onto warmed tortillas and top with pickled cabbage, sliced red onion, avocado slices, dollops of guacamole and a scattering of coriander. Squeeze over lime wedges, roll up and devour.

Korean-style Sloppy Sliders

◎ Serves 4

🕔 5 minutes

🍲 25 minutes

Ridiculously indulgent and ideal weekend fare, these sliders are pepped up with Asian kitchen staples. I've suggested sriracha for spice here but if you have a tub of gochujang in the fridge waiting to be used up, use that instead.

1 tbsp groundnut (peanut)
  or vegetable oil
Bunch of spring onions (scallions),
  thinly sliced
1 large carrot, julienned
2 garlic cloves, finely grated
500g (1lb 2oz) minced (ground)
  beef (15% fat)
2 tbsp soft dark brown sugar
2 tbsp soy sauce
1 tbsp sesame oil
2 tbsp rice vinegar
5 tbsp sriracha
12 brioche slider burger buns
3 tbsp toasted sesame seeds

For the pickled chilli cucumber

½ cucumber, peeled, deseeded
  and cut into half-moons
1 green finger chilli, thinly sliced
75ml (⅓ cup) rice wine vinegar
75ml (⅓ cup) water
1 star anise
2 tbsp caster (superfine) sugar

For the burger sauce

1-2 tbsp sriracha (or to your level
  of spiciness)
6 tbsp mayonnaise

1 Heat the oil in a frying pan (skillet) and gently fry the spring onions (save a handful to garnish), carrot and garlic for 5 minutes until tender. Add the minced beef and increase the heat to brown all over.

2 Add the sugar, soy sauce, sesame oil, rice vinegar, sriracha and a splash of water and bubble gently for 20 minutes, adding a splash more water if it starts to get too dry.

3 Meanwhile, put the cucumber and chilli in a bowl. Pour the vinegar into a small pan with the same amount of water and the star anise and sugar. Heat until the sugar has dissolved, then pour the hot pickling liquid over the cucumber and chilli and set aside for at least 10 minutes.

4 To make the burger sauce, mix the sriracha and mayonnaise until combined.

5 Toast the brioche buns, spread with the sriracha mayo and fill with the sticky mince. Scatter with the remaining spring onions, top with the pickled cucumber, toasted sesame seeds and serve.

Alphabet Soup & Grilled Cheese

◎ Serves 6

⏱ 5 minutes

🍲 45 minutes

🅥🅔 Vegetarian

Recipes like this one are steeped in nostalgia for me and although I attempt to better my cooking skills year on year, I always find my way back to tomato soup with grilled cheese. It's grub that would have seen us through our teens, but in Ireland would have looked more like spaghetti hoops with buttered toast. Not wanting to deprive my kids of this particular joy, I present alphabet soup with a pretty spectacular mozza-loaded grilled cheese toastie. Alphabet pasta should be easy to track down but any short pasta, or even orzo, will do the trick.

2 red onions, cut into wedges
1 whole garlic bulb, cloves
  separated but left unpeeled
2 carrots, peeled and roughly
  chopped
2 small leeks, sliced into thick coins
400g (14oz) vine tomatoes, halved
200g (7oz) butternut squash,
  peeled, deseeded and cut
  into small cubes
3 tbsp olive oil
1 litre (4 cups) fresh vegetable stock
150g (5oz) alphabet pasta
Sea salt and freshly ground
  black pepper
190g (7oz) jar of green pesto
Fresh basil leaves, to serve

For the grilled cheese

6 small slices of sourdough
1 garlic clove
1 tbsp extra virgin olive oil
150g (5oz) mozzarella, grated

1 Preheat the oven to 200°C/180°C fan/400°F/Gas 6. Toss the onions, garlic, veggies and olive oil in a large roasting tray. Season well and roast for 35–40 minutes, turning occasionally, until lovely and tender and roasted. Leave the oven on for the grilled cheese.

2 Tip the veg into a large pan, squeezing the garlic out of the skins. Cover with the stock and place over a medium-high heat. When it comes to the boil add the pasta and simmer gently until the pasta is tender.

3 Meanwhile, toast the bread slices and rub all over with the cut garlic clove. Place on a baking sheet, drizzle with oil and scatter with the cheese. Pop into the oven for 4–5 minutes until the cheese is melted and bubbling.

4 Serve the soup with the melted mozzarella toasts, a dollop of pesto and a scattering of basil.

Prep it Ahead, Cook it Later

Roast Cherry Tomato Pici

◎ Serves 4–6

⬠ 30 minutes, plus chilling

▭ 40–50 minutes

Ⓥ Vegetarian

I apologise to my regular readers, who have seen variants of this recipe throughout my cookbooks. It started as a cheap dinner for two but now it's become a staple part of our regular weeknight family meals. The idea is to roast sweet cherry tomatoes and garlic until their flavour intensifies and then press together with a fork in the roasting tray to create the perfect coating for freshly cooked pasta. In this version, we make our own pici, one of the easiest pastas to make which can be made in the time the sauce cooks.

600g (1lb 5oz) cherry tomatoes
1 whole garlic bulb, cloves
   separated and left unpeeled
Handful of thyme sprigs
Pinch of chilli flakes
2 tbsp olive oil
2 × 100g (3½oz) burrata balls,
   roughly torn
50g (2oz) Parmesan cheese (or
   vegetarian alternative), grated
Extra virgin olive oil, for drizzling
Sea salt and freshly ground
   black pepper
Basil leaves, to serve

For the pici

500g (4 cups) white bread flour
2 tbsp extra virgin olive oil
1 tsp fine sea salt
240ml (1 cup) lukewarm water

1. Make the pici. Mix the flour, oil and salt with enough lukewarm water to bring it together into a dough (you may not need all of it). Shape into a ball and knead for 5–10 minutes until smooth. Press into a disc, wrap in cling film and chill for 30 minutes (or overnight if you want to get ahead).

2. Meanwhile, preheat the oven to 200°/180°C/400°F/Gas 6. Toss the tomatoes, garlic cloves, thyme sprigs, chilli flakes and olive oil in a roasting tray, season well and roast for 30–45 minutes until tender and broken down. Slip the garlic cloves out of their papery skins and remove and discard the thyme sprigs, then mash everything together with a fork.

3. Meanwhile, press the dough into a flat rectangle and cut into pieces each about 15g (½oz) each. Keep them under a damp tea towel while you work. With lightly oiled hands, roll each piece out into long noodles, about the thickness of a straw or biro.

4. Bring a large pan of salted water to the boil and cook the wiggly pici for 4–5 minutes. Drain and return to the pan, then toss with the tomato sauce over a low heat.

5. Serve with the burrata, plenty of Parmesan, a drizzle of extra virgin olive oil, black pepper and some torn basil leaves.

Slow-roast Chicken Shawarma Platter

◎ Serves 6

⏱ 15 minutes, plus marinating

🍲 2–2 ½ hours

When we lived in east Los Angeles we were spoiled for choice when it came to Middle Eastern restaurants. Flame-licked meats served with hummus, toum (the addictive lemony garlic sauce), lavash, seasonal vegetables and fresh herbs – it was such a treat. This recipe recreates just some of the elements of those wonderful feasts. The chicken really benefits from the marinating time, if you can prepare it in advance. Toast the flatbreads over an open flame with tongs for best results.

1 large free-range chicken
  (about 1.8kg/4lb)
2 red onions, cut into wedges
2 tbsp olive oil, for drizzling
Juice of 1 lemon
2 × 400g (14oz) tins chickpeas,
  drained and rinsed

For the tahini yoghurt

250g (9oz) natural yoghurt
1 garlic clove, grated
1 tbsp tahini

For the spice blend

1 tsp ground coriander
1 tsp ground turmeric
1 tbsp ground cumin
1 tsp sweet smoked paprika
½ tsp ground cinnamon
¼ tsp ground cardamom (or the
  ground seeds from 6 pods)

To serve

⅔ cucumber, peeled, deseeded
  and diced
150g (5oz) cherry tomatoes,
  quartered
Handful of coriander (cilantro)
  leaves
6 warmed flatbreads
2 baby gem lettuces, shredded
Sea salt and freshly ground
  black pepper

1   Mix all the ingredients for the spice blend together and rub all over the chicken. Leave to marinate at room temperature for 30 minutes, or overnight in the fridge if you like (take it out 30 minutes before roasting).

2   Preheat the oven to 160°C/140°C fan/325°F/Gas 3. Scatter the red onion wedges over the bottom of a roasting tray, place the chicken on top and drizzle with olive oil. Squeeze over the lemon juice and pop the halves in the cavity of the chicken. Roast slowly for 2–2½ hours (cover with foil if it starts to get too dark).

3   Blend the yoghurt, garlic and tahini together and set aside.

4   When the chicken is cooked, remove from the oven and place on a warmed platter. Pour any juices and onions from the roasting tray into a frying pan (skillet), add the chickpeas and warm through over a low heat.

5   Toss the cucumber, tomatoes and coriander together in a bowl and season. Serve the chicken and chickpeas at the table with warmed flatbreads, tahini yoghurt, the cucumber and tomatoes and shredded lettuce alongside.

Braised Beef Shin Lasagne

◎ Serves 8

⏱ 30 minutes

🍲 3–3½ hours

Lasagne was one of the first things I learned to cook and it still remains one of my favourite comfort food dishes. This version yields next-level results. I've used braised beef shin, cooked gently until quiveringly tender, which makes all the difference to the ragu, which is then layered between pasta and a rich cheese sauce.

2kg (4lb 8oz) beef shin, cut into pieces
3 tbsp plain (all-purpose) flour, seasoned
4–5 tbsp olive oil
1 large onion, finely chopped
250g (9oz) chestnut mushrooms, finely chopped
3 garlic cloves, grated
1 bay leaf
5 sprigs of fresh oregano, leaves stripped
2 tbsp tomato purée (paste)
450ml (1¾ cups) good red wine
200ml (generous ¾ cup) fresh beef stock
400g (14oz) tin chopped tomatoes
2 tsp red wine vinegar
12 sheets of fresh lasagne pasta
Mixed leaves, to serve

For the cheese sauce

75g (3oz) butter
75g (3oz) plain (all-purpose) flour
800ml (generous 3 cups) whole milk
150g (5oz) Cheddar cheese, grated
100g (3½oz) Parmesan cheese, grated
1 teaspoon Dijon mustard

1 To make the filling, toss the beef in the seasoned flour. Heat a good layer of oil in a casserole and fry the beef, in batches if necessary, until really browned on all sides. Transfer to a plate.

2 Add the onion and mushrooms with a little more oil to the casserole and fry for 10 minutes until golden, then add the garlic, herbs and tomato purée. Pour in the wine, bring to the boil and bubble for 2–3 minutes. Add the stock, chopped tomatoes and vinegar and return the beef to the pan. Reduce to a simmer and cook gently, partially covered, for 2½–3 hours until the meat is really tender and falls apart when you push it with a spoon.

3 Meanwhile make the cheese sauce. Melt the butter in a pan and stir in the flour and cook for a minute or two then gradually add the milk until you have a smooth, thick sauce. Season well and add most of the cheese (saving some for scattering on top) and the mustard.

4 Once the beef is tender, remove the bay leaf and shred the meat into the sauce. If the sauce is looking a little juicy you can reduce it until it just coats the meat.

5 Preheat the oven to 200°C/180°C fan/400°F/Gas 6. Spoon a third of the meat into a large ovenproof dish, then top with 4 of the lasagne sheets and spoon over a third of the cheese sauce. Repeat the layers twice more, ending with cheese sauce. Scatter with the rest of the cheese and bake for 30–35 minutes until bubbling and golden. Serve with a green salad.

Jerk Chicken with Mango Salsa

◎ Serves 4–6

🫙 20 minutes, plus marinating

🍲 20 minutes

This really comes into its own when cooked over hot coals, ensuring not only a hit of heat but also the essential smoky element that really good jerk chicken is all about. If you're feeling fancy place the mango over the hot coals of a barbecue until you have deep char marks all over, before prepping the salsa.

5 spring onions (scallions), trimmed
2 scotch bonnet chillies, roughly chopped
4 garlic cloves
3cm (1in) piece of fresh ginger, peeled and grated
1 tsp ground allspice
¼ tsp ground nutmeg
½ tsp ground cinnamon
1 tsp dried oregano
6 sprigs of fresh thyme, leaves stripped
Juice of 1 lime
2 tbsp tomato ketchup
3 tbsp soy sauce
8 free-range chicken thighs (bone in and skin on)
Sea salt and freshly ground black pepper

For the coconut rice

350g (12oz) long grain rice, rinsed
400ml (1¾ cups) tin coconut milk
225ml (scant 1 cup) water

For the salsa

1 large ripe mango, peeled, stoned and finely chopped
½ cucumber, peeled, deseeded and finely chopped
Juice of 1 lime
1 tbsp extra virgin olive oil
Good handful of roughly chopped fresh coriander (cilantro)

1 In a small food processor whizz the spring onions, chillies, garlic, ginger, spices and herbs to form a paste. Add the lime juice, ketchup and soy sauce and plenty of seasoning.

2 Put the chicken into a large ziplock bag and pour in the marinade. Seal the bag and give it a good shake until everything is completely combined and the chicken is evenly coated. Leave in the fridge to marinate for at least 2 hours, or overnight if you have the time. Remove the chicken from the fridge 30 minutes before you are ready to cook.

3 Preheat the oven to 200°C/180°C fan/400°F/Gas 6. Put the rice into a pan with the coconut milk and water. Add a good pinch of salt and cover. Bring to the boil, then reduce the heat and simmer for 15 minutes until the rice is tender and the liquid has been absorbed. Leave it to stand with the lid on until you're ready to serve.

4 Combine all the ingredients for the salsa and season well.

5 Heat a large ovenproof frying pan (skillet) over a medium-high heat (crack a window open or you will end up coughing from the chilli!) and fry the chicken pieces for 3–4 minutes each side until charred and golden. Transfer to the oven for 10 minutes until they are cooked through. Serve with the coconut rice and salsa.

Prep it Ahead, Cook it Later

Prep it Ahead, Cook it Later

Crispy Chicken Parmesan with Hidden Veg Tomato Sauce

◎ Serves 4 (with double sauce so freeze half)

🖐 15 minutes

🍲 55 minutes

This sauce is so simple to make that making double is no effort at all. Pop half in the freezer so you have it on standby, either to make the dish again or just to fold through pasta with grated Parmesan.

1 First make the sauce. Preheat the oven to 200°C/180°C fan/400°F/Gas 6. In a large roasting tray, toss the vegetables with the olive oil, garlic cloves, chilli flakes and oregano. Season well and roast for 40 minutes, tossing once, until tender and golden.

2 While the veg roasts, place the chicken breasts between two pieces of baking parchment and bash with a rolling pin until they are about 1cm (½in) thick. Put the seasoned flour, beaten egg and breadcrumbs mixed with Parmesan into three separate dishes.

3 Remove the roasted veg from the oven and then increase the temperature to the highest it will go. Squeeze the garlic cloves from their skin and tip the veg into a food processor, add the tinned tomatoes and a tin full of water and blitz till smooth.

4 Heat the sunflower oil in a large ovenproof sauté pan (skillet) over a high heat. Dip the chicken in the flour then the egg and then the cheesy crumbs and fry the chicken in the oil for 2 minutes either side until golden brown (they will continue to cook in the oven). Remove and transfer to a plate and wipe out any remaining oil from the pan.

5 Pour half of the blitzed sauce into the pan and bubble over a medium heat for 10 minutes until it has reduced slightly. Nestle the fried chicken into the sauce and scatter with the grated mozzarella.

6 Transfer to the oven for 4–5 minutes until the mozzarella is melted, then serve with freshly cooked spaghetti.

2 large free-range chicken breasts
1 tbsp plain (all-purpose) flour, seasoned
1 large free-range egg, beaten
50g (2oz) fine dry breadcrumbs (use panko for best results)
3 heaped tbsp Parmesan cheese, finely grated
150ml (scant ⅔ cup) sunflower oil
75g (3oz) mozzarella, grated
Cooked spaghetti, to serve

For the hidden veg tomato sauce

1 red onion, finely chopped
2 celery sticks, chopped
1 large leek, sliced
2 courgettes (zucchini), sliced
2 carrots, peeled and chopped
300g (10oz) vine tomatoes, halved
3–4 tbsp olive oil
1 whole bulb garlic, cloves separated
½ tsp dried red chilli flakes
½ tsp dried oregano
400g (14oz) tin plum tomatoes
Sea salt and freshly ground black pepper

Grandad's Kleftiko

◎ Serves 6

🍶 30 minutes, plus marinating

🍲 3 hours

A classic roast lamb dish from Greece that wound up becoming a regular staple of my grandmother's kitchen repertoire as it was a favourite of my Grandad's. It's one of those simple dishes that is more than the sum of its parts and with minimal effort you get mouth-watering results: tender lamb with a rich cooking liquor that is ideal to douse the meat with. I like to pair this with a fresh Greek salad but you could also serve with couscous for more substance.

2kg (4lb 8oz) lamb shoulder
1 large onion, sliced into thin wedges
1 red (bell) pepper, deseeded and sliced
1 bay leaf
1 cinnamon stick
5 sprigs of fresh oregano
1 whole bulb of garlic, cut in half through the middle
Pared zest of 1 lemon and juice of ½
200ml (generous ¾ cup) white wine
4 tbsp olive oil
600g (1lb 5oz) waxy potatoes
200ml (generous ¾ cup) chicken stock
300g (10oz) medium vine tomatoes, quartered
Sea salt and freshly ground black pepper

1   Put the lamb into a dish with all the ingredients except for the potatoes, stock and tomatoes. Season well and leave to marinate for at least 2 hours.

2   Preheat the oven to 160°C/140°C fan/325°F/Gas 3. Line a large roasting tray with baking parchment so it hangs over all sides. Put the potatoes in the bottom of the tray then top with the lamb and all the marinade. Add the stock and tomatoes then wrap the sides of the parchment over the top.

3   Cover the whole tray with foil and roast for 2½ hours. Uncover the dish, increase the temperature to 220°C/200°C fan/425°F/Gas 7 and roast for a further 30 minutes until really tender, juicy and golden.

THE BEST MEALS ARE SHARED WITH FAMILY AND FRIENDS.

Cheesy Schnitzel with Root Veg Mash

◎ Serves 4

⏱ 20 minutes

⏲ 20 minutes

Unadulterated crispy breadcrumbed cheesy goodness – if that doesn't sell it to you I don't know what will! This retro classic uses pork loin steaks in place of chicken. A splodge of lingonberry jam (my wife's favourite) provides tart sweetness if you can track it down in the food section of a ubiquitous Swedish furniture store. Japanese panko breadcrumbs are available in most supermarkets these days and are well worth throwing in your trolley for recipes just like this.

For the schnitzel

4 pork loin steaks, about 175g (6oz) each, cut in half and beaten until thin
2 heaped tsp Dijon mustard
8 slices of Gruyère cheese
4 slices of smoked ham
20g (¾oz) butter
1 tbsp olive oil
Lingonberry jam, to serve
Handful of chopped flat-leaf parsley, to serve

For the coating

3 tbsp plain (all-purpose) flour, seasoned
2 free-range medium eggs, lightly beaten
100g (3½oz) panko breadcrumbs

For the root veg mash

500g (1lb 2oz) floury potatoes, peeled and cubed
2 parsnips, peeled and cubed
300g (10oz) butternut squash, peeled and diced
600ml (2½ cups) whole milk
30g (1oz) butter
1 tbsp extra virgin olive oil
Small handful of finely chopped chives
Sea salt and freshly ground black pepper

1   First, dollop and spread Dijon mustard on each piece of pork, then place a slice of cheese, followed by a slice of ham and a slice of cheese. Add another piece of the meat over the cheese and press down.

2   Dip each pork steak first in flour, then beaten egg, then breadcrumbs, pressing to get an even coating. Set aside on a plate while you prepare the mash, or cover with cling film and put into the fridge if you are preparing ahead.

3   Put the potatoes, parsnips and squash in a large pan of cold salted water. Cover and bring to a steady boil, then simmer for 12–15 minutes, or until they are tender when pierced with a fork.

4   Heat the milk and butter in a small pan until the butter is melted. Drain the root veg and push through a ricer into a bowl (or use a potato masher to mash until as smooth as you can get). Stir in the warm milk and butter mixture and mix until smooth. Season with salt and pepper and stir through the olive oil and chives.

5   Meanwhile, melt the butter and oil in a pan over a medium-high heat and fry the schnitzels for 6 minutes each side, or until golden brown and cooked through.

6   Serve each schnitzel with a generous dollop of velvety root veg mash, lingonberry jam and a sprinkle of chopped parsley.

④ EASY FAVOURITES

Falafel Plate with Shaved Salad, Garlic & Mint Yoghurt & Harissa

◎ Makes 20

🏷 20 minutes, plus overnight soaking

🍲 20 minutes

(VE) Vegetarian

Falafel with all the trimmings! Gram flour gives the falafel both taste and texture but if you can't track it down you can use plain flour instead.

250g (9oz) dried chickpeas, soaked overnight
2 garlic cloves, grated
1 small onion, finely chopped
2 tsp ground cumin
1 tsp ground coriander
Good pinch of chilli powder
3 tbsp chopped coriander (cilantro)
2 tbsp chopped flat-leaf parsley
1 tsp baking powder
2 tbsp gram flour (chickpea flour)
1 litre (4 cups) neutral oil (groundnut/peanut or sunflower), for frying
Sea salt and freshly ground black pepper

For the salad

1 fennel bulb
¼ white cabbage
½ large cucumber, deseeded
Juice of 1 lemon
1 tsp cumin seeds
Good drizzle of extra virgin olive oil

To serve

250g (9oz) Greek yoghurt
Garlic cloves, grated
1 tbsp finely chopped fresh mint
Dollops of rose harissa
Pitta breads or flatbreads, warmed

1   Drain the chickpeas and tip into a food processor with all the ingredients except the oil. Add plenty of salt and pepper and pulse to combine, adding a tablespoon or two of water if needed just to help it to come together (but you want it to stay as dry as possible).

2   For the salad, shave the fennel as thinly as possible and tip into a bowl. Slice the cabbage very thinly and add to the fennel. Shred the cucumber with a julienne peeler or normal potato peeler and add to the bowl. Toss with the lemon juice, cumin seeds and lots of olive oil. Season well and set aside.

3   Mix the yoghurt with the garlic and mint. Season to taste and set aside.

4   Heat the neutral oil in a heavy-based high-sided pan to 170°C/340°F (if you don't have a kitchen thermometer drop a pea-sized amount of the mixture into the oil; if it sizzles immediately it is ready). Use two spoons to form smooth dollops (quenelles) of the falafel mixture and drop them into the pan, working in small batches to prevent overcrowding. Fry for 3–4 minutes until golden all over. Scoop out and drain on kitchen paper. Serve warm with the salad, yoghurt, harissa and warm bread.

Chicken & Cheddar Cobbler Pie

◎ Serves 4

🕐 20 minutes

🍲 40 minutes

A simplified version of the classic comfort food chicken pot pie which replaces the pastry element with a far easier to make cobbler topping to streamline the cooking process. An ideal recipe for when you have loads of guests coming over or a simple solution to a midweek supper. It's also a perfect dish to make with leftover chicken. If you want to make this ahead, prep the filling in advance and store in the fridge. When you're ready to cook add the cobbler topping and you've got a meal in minutes.

75g (3oz) butter
125g (4oz) drained pickled
   pearl onions
1 large carrot, finely diced
2 sprigs of thyme, leaves stripped
2 tbsp plain (all-purpose) flour
500ml (2 cups) chicken stock
2 tsp Dijon mustard
150ml (scant ⅔ cup) single cream
1 rotisserie chicken, torn into bite-
   sized pieces
150g (5oz) purple sprouting
   broccoli, stalks chopped, florets
   left whole or halved if large
100g (3½oz) baby spinach

For the dumplings

225g (8oz) cold butter, cubed
475g (3¾ cups) self-raising flour
100g (3½oz) Irish Cheddar, grated
1–2 tbsp water
Sea salt and freshly ground
   black pepper

1   Preheat the oven to 200°C/180°C fan/400°F/Gas 6. Melt the butter in a medium-sized ovenproof casserole, add the pickled onions and carrot and fry gently for 5 minutes, or until softened with a little colour. Add the thyme leaves and flour to the buttery vegetables and cook for minute, stirring all the time.

2   Gradually add the stock, whisking briskly until it thickens. If it goes a little lumpy, don't worry; just whisk vigorously until it becomes smooth.

3   Season well and add the mustard. Pour in the cream and stir through along with the chicken, broccoli and spinach. Let the spinach wilt as you simmer for a minute then set aside.

4   Make the dumplings by rubbing the butter and flour together in a bowl until it resembles breadcrumbs, then add most of the cheese and season. Briskly mix 1–2 tablespoons of cold water into the mixture with a knife then bring it all together into a ball using your hands. Knead slightly, before forming into 20 dumplings, each around the size of a golf ball.

5   Arrange the dumplings on top of the chicken mix in the casserole, starting from the outside and leaving a little space in between each one to allow for rising. Work your way to the inside to give a nice pattern. Sprinkle over the remaining cheese and bake in the oven for 25 minutes until the dumplings are risen and golden.

Veggie-packed Yuk Sung

○ Serves 4–6

🍶 20 minutes

🍲 10 minutes

VE Vegetarian

Typically yuk sung uses tinned water chestnuts but if you can't track them down simply leave them out; alternatively peel, deseed and dice a cucumber to add that crunch element.

100g (3½oz) vermicelli noodles
1 tbsp groundnut (peanut) or
  vegetable oil
3 garlic cloves, grated
3cm (1in) piece of fresh ginger,
  peeled and grated
Bunch of spring onions (scallions),
  thinly sliced
1 red chilli, finely chopped
2 carrots, very finely chopped
300g (10oz) oyster or shiitake
  mushrooms, thinly sliced
225g (8oz) water chestnuts,
  finely chopped
400g (14oz) quorn mince (or you
  can use turkey or pork mince)
1½ tsp Chinese five-spice
3 tbsp soy sauce
2 tbsp honey
1 tbsp rice wine vinegar
1 tbsp sesame oil
2–3 baby gem lettuces
Coriander (cilantro) leaves,
  to garnish

1 Crush the noodles in your hands, put into a bowl and cover with boiling water. Leave to soak and soften while you cook the rest of the filling.

2 Heat the oil in a wok or large frying pan (skillet) over a high heat and fry the garlic, ginger, half the spring onions and the chilli for a minute until fragrant. Add the carrots, mushrooms and water chestnuts and fry for a further 4–5 minutes until they have softened and reduced in volume. Add the quorn mince and five-spice and toss together.

3 Blend the soy sauce, honey, vinegar and sesame oil together and pour into the wok. Cook for a few minutes more while you drain the noodles.

4 Separate the lettuce leaves and fill them with a little bit of noodles and the mince mixture. Garnish with the rest of the spring onions and coriander leaves and serve.

Mushroom & Cauliflower Ragu Lasagne

○ Serves 6–8

⌚ 20 minutes

🍲 1½ hours

Ⓥ Vegetarian

A rich veggie-based lasagne that yields delicious results. You can pulse the mushrooms and cauli in a food processor to speed up the prepping process.

1 Make the ragu: heat the oil in a large pan and add the garlic and mushrooms and cook over a medium-high heat for 5 minutes until golden brown. Tip out of the pan and set aside.

2 Add the butter to the pan and fry the onion and chopped cauliflower leaves until softened, then add the grated cauliflower, rosemary and chilli flakes and return the mushrooms to the pan.

3 Add the wine and cook for 2–3 minutes, then add the tomatoes, tomato purée and stock. Season and simmer for 45 minutes until rich and thick. Stir in the parsley.

4 Meanwhile make the béchamel. Melt the butter in a pan and add the flour and cook for a minute or two. Then gradually add the milk until you have a thick, glossy sauce. Season well and add plenty of nutmeg. Stir in almost all the grated cheeses, saving some for the top. Preheat the oven to 200°C/180°C fan/400°F/Gas 6.

5 Spoon one-third of the ragu into a large ovenproof dish, then top with 2–3 lasagne sheets and one-third of the béchamel. Repeat twice more, ending with a layer of béchamel and the last of the grated cheese.

6 Bake for 40 minutes until golden and bubbling then serve with a bitter leaf salad.

3 tbsp olive oil
3 garlic cloves, thinly sliced
500g (1lb 2oz) chestnut mushrooms, finely chopped
25g (1oz) unsalted butter
1 large onion, thinly sliced
1 medium cauliflower (about 600g/1lb 5oz), coarsely grated, leaves roughly chopped
3 sprigs of rosemary
Good pinch of chilli flakes
200ml (generous ¾ cup) red or white wine
400g (14oz) tin chopped tomatoes
1 tbsp tomato purée (paste)
450ml (1¾ cups) hot vegetable stock
Handful of finely chopped flat-leaf parsley
6–12 fresh lasagne sheets (depending on size)
Sea salt and freshly ground black pepper
Bitter leaf salad, to serve

For the béchamel

60g (2¼oz) butter
60g (2¼oz) plain (all-purpose) flour
600ml (2½ cups) whole milk
Good grating of fresh nutmeg
70g (2¾oz) Gruyère cheese (or vegetarian alternative), grated
120g (4oz) Cheddar cheese (or vegetarian alternative), grated

Beef Hot Pot with Dumplings

◎ Serves 4

🍶 30 minutes

🍲 3 hours

Serious levels of warmth and comfort will be found bubbling beneath the lid of this winter warmer. The stew itself is best made in advance and the dumplings added before you are ready to serve. Use the best-quality ingredients you can for this dish to really make it sing.

2 tbsp olive oil
1kg (2lb 4oz) braising steak such as bavette/flank or shin, cut into large pieces
2 tbsp plain (all-purpose) flour
1 onion, sliced
2 large carrots, peeled and diced
3 garlic cloves, grated
3 sprigs of thyme
200ml (generous ¾ cup) red wine
500ml (2 cups) beef stock
Sea salt and freshly ground black pepper

For the dumplings

250g (2 cups) self-raising flour
2 tbsp chopped flat-leaf parsley
100g (3½oz) butter
50g (2oz) Cheddar cheese, grated
100ml (scant ½ cup) milk

1   Preheat the oven to 180°C/160°C fan/350°F/Gas 4. Heat the olive oil in a large casserole over a medium-high heat. While it is heating, toss the beef in the flour and season well with salt and pepper.

2   Add the beef and fry until brown on all sides. Remove from the casserole and set aside.

3   Add the onion, carrot, garlic and thyme to the casserole with a little more oil if needed and gently fry for 5–6 minutes until softened.

4   Add the red wine and bubble to reduce almost by half before returning the beef to the casserole with the stock. Cover and put in the oven for 2½ hours.

5   When it has almost finished cooking, make the dumplings. Add the flour, parsley and butter to a large bowl with the Cheddar. Use your fingertips to rub the butter into the flour until it resembles rough breadcrumbs. Season well and gradually add the milk into the mix. Tip out onto a flour surface and knead a little before rolling into a sausage shape. Divide into 12 pieces and use lightly floured hands to shape into balls.

6   Shred the beef a little and stir through the sauce. Arrange the dumplings on top, leaving a little gap between each one. Cover and return to the oven for 30 minutes until the dumplings have risen, then remove the lid and cook for another 15 minutes until they're golden.

Spiced Salmon with Pineapple Salsa & Caramelised Onion Rice

◎ Serves 8

🫙 10 minutes, plus marinating

🍲 45 minutes

A spicy fishy feast for the whole family. This recipe feeds a crowd but you can scale it down if you like by using individual salmon fillets.

1kg (2lb 4oz) side of salmon
2 tbsp maple syrup
1 tbsp smoked paprika
2 tsp ground cumin
Generous pinch of cayenne pepper

For the salsa

1 medium pineapple, peeled and
   chopped into small chunks
1 red chilli, deseeded and finely
   chopped
Juice of 1 lime
2 tbsp olive oil
Good handful of roughly chopped
   coriander (cilantro)
Sea salt and freshly ground
   black pepper

For the caramelised onion rice

2 tbsp olive oil
2 large onions, thinly sliced
500g (1lb 2oz) basmati rice, rinsed
1 tsp dried thyme
A good handful of coriander,
   roughly chopped

1 Put the salmon into a large dish. Mix the maple syrup and spices together, then spread evenly all over the salmon. Leave in the fridge to marinate for at least 2 hours, or overnight if you have the time.

2 Combine all the salsa ingredients except for the coriander in a bowl and season with salt and pepper.

3 For the rice, heat the oil in a large pan and fry the onions over a medium heat for 12–15 minutes, stirring, until caramelised and sticky. Stir in the rice and then pour over 1 litre (4 cups) of water and season with salt and pepper. Cover and bring to the boil, then reduce the heat and simmer for 12 minutes. Remove from the heat and leave to stand, covered, for 5 minutes. Fluff up with a fork and stir in the herbs.

4 Meanwhile, preheat the grill to high. Line the grill tray with foil and grease well then place the salmon, skin-side up, on the tray. Grill for 3–4 minutes until the skin is crispy then flip over and grill for 5 minutes until just cooked and golden brown.

5 Stir the coriander through the salsa. Serve the salmon with the salsa and caramelised onion rice.

TASTE AS YOU GO,
IT REALLY DOES
MAKE A DIFFERENCE
TO THE FINAL MEAL TO
TASTE AT EACH STAGE.

Crispy Egg Fried Rice Bowls

◎ Serves 4

🥫 10 minutes

🍲 15 minutes

A Kylie Kwong egg method that I revisit time and time again for its instant appeal – crispy edges and stunningly runny yolk. The perfect topping to simple veggie-packed fried rice. You will get the very best results if you refrigerate the cooked and cooled rice overnight.

250g (9oz) jasmine or basmati rice, rinsed well
100ml (3½fl oz) groundnut (peanut) oil
225g (8oz) firm tofu (smoked if you can find it), cut into 1.5cm (½in) cubes
2 garlic cloves, thinly sliced
6 spring onions (scallions), thinly sliced
1 carrot, finely chopped
125g (4oz) frozen peas, defrosted
2 tsp soy sauce
2 tsp toasted sesame oil
4 large free-range eggs
3 tbsp oyster sauce
1 red chilli, thinly sliced
2 tsp toasted sesame seeds
Sea salt and freshly ground black pepper

1   Tip the rinsed rice into a pan and cover with 600ml (2½ cups) cold water. Season well with salt, cover and bring to the boil. Reduce the heat and cook for 12 minutes, then drain and rinse under cold water to make sure the grains are separated. Fluff up the grains of rice with a fork.

2   Meanwhile, heat 2 tablespoons of the oil in a large wok and fry the tofu for 6–7 minutes over a high heat until golden and crisp. Add the garlic and toss well until the garlic turns light gold, then tip onto a plate. Add another tablespoon of oil to the pan and fry half the spring onions and the carrot for 2–3 minutes. Return the tofu to the pan, add the peas and cooked rice and toss well; cook for a minute more. Drizzle with the soy sauce and sesame oil and spoon into a warm bowl.

3   Heat the remaining oil in the wok and when smoking hot add the eggs; cook for a minute until the edges are all bubbly and golden and crisp. Remove with a slotted spoon and drain on kitchen paper.

4   Divide the rice between four bowls and top each with an egg. Drizzle with the oyster sauce, scatter with the chilli, sesame seeds and remaining sliced spring onion and serve.

Ricotta Gnocchi with Wild Mushrooms

◎ Serves 6

🍶 30 minutes

🍲 15 minutes

Ⓥ Vegetarian

One of my favourite Irish food writers Rory O'Connell has a recipe for something similar in his cookbook *The Joy of Food* using chanterelles. Gnocchi made with potato can often be a step too far for some, but do give this ricotta version a go for the lightest and most delicate little dumplings. If fresh wild mushrooms aren't available you can use dried wild mushrooms instead. Soak in boiling water for 10 minutes, drain, weigh and then make up with chestnut mushrooms.

2 tbsp olive oil
25g (1oz) butter
4 large garlic cloves, thinly sliced
400g (14oz) mixed chestnut and fresh wild mushrooms (chanterelle, girolle etc.)
2 sprigs of thyme, leaves picked
200ml (generous ¾ cup) white wine
1 tbsp Dijon mustard
300ml (1¼ cups) fresh vegetable stock
200ml (generous ¾ cup) double (heavy) cream
300g (10oz) baby spinach
Squeeze of lemon juice
2 tbsp finely chopped flat-leaf parsley
Extra virgin olive oil, for drizzling
1 tbsp finely chopped dill
Shavings of pecorino (or vegetarian alternative), to serve

For the gnocchi

500g (1lb 2oz) fresh ricotta (or vegetarian alternative)
100g (3½oz) pecorino, finely grated
250g (2 cups) plain (all-purpose) flour
4 medium free-range eggs
Sea salt and freshly ground black pepper

1   Mix all the ingredients for the gnocchi together and season well with sea salt and freshly ground black pepper. Divide the mix in half and roll into long sausages, about 2.5cm (1in) thick. Slice with a sharp knife into 2cm (¾in) thick slices and place them on a lightly floured tray while you make the sauce.

2   Heat the oil and butter in a large pan and fry the garlic for a couple of minutes. Add the mushrooms and thyme and fry over a high heat for 4–5 minutes until browned and slightly crisp. Season well, then splash in the wine and bubble for a minute or two.

3   Add the mustard, and stock, bubble together for 3–4 minutes until thickened, then add the cream, spinach, lemon juice and the parsley.

4   Meanwhile, bring a large pan of salted water to the boil, cook the gnocchi in batches for 2–3 minutes, or until they float to the surface. Remove with a slotted spoon and add to the mushroom sauce.

5   Divide between plates and drizzle with extra virgin olive oil. Scatter with the dill and the pecorino shavings and serve.

Easy Favourites

Mac 'n' Peas

◎ Serves 4

⬚ 10 minutes

⬚ 30 minutes

(VE) Vegetarian

This pesto is great with other green veggies – you can try it with a mix of frozen broad beans and peas, or swap in half for raw broccoli florets.

1   Preheat the oven to 200°C/180°C fan/400°F/Gas 6. Cook the pasta in boiling salted water for 10 minutes until not quite cooked. Drain and set aside.

2   Meanwhile, in a small food processor, blitz the peas with the garlic, basil, mint, pine nuts and the extra virgin olive oil. Whizz in the mascarpone and the Parmesan.

3   Melt the butter in a pan, add the flour and cook for 2 minutes, then gradually add the vegetable stock until you have a smooth, thick sauce. Add the pesto and stir until smooth. Season to taste.

4   Stir the sauce through the pasta and tip into an ovenproof dish. Scatter with the rest of the Parmesan and the grated mozzarella and bake for 20–25 minutes until bubbling and golden.

350g (12oz) macaroni
200g (7oz) frozen peas, defrosted
1 garlic clove
50g (2oz) basil leaves
15g (½oz) mint leaves
30g (1oz) toasted pine nuts
3 tbsp extra virgin olive oil
100g (3½oz) mascarpone
50g (2oz) Parmesan cheese (or vegetarian alternative), grated, plus extra to scatter
25g (1oz) unsalted butter
25g (1oz) plain (all-purpose) flour
400ml (1¾ cups) vegetable stock
75g (3oz) mozzarella, grated

Sage-roasted Butternut Squash with Whipped Goats' Cheese & Brown Butter Tortellini

◎ Serves 4

⬟ 5 minutes

▢ 40 minutes

VE Vegetarian

A rather bougie way of zhuzhing up shop-bought ingredients with fabulous results (most of the ingredients for this recipe can be bunged into a shopping trolley on the way home from work). The whipped goats' cheese also works well as a dip; add a little cream cheese if you prefer a milder flavour and then top it with oven-roasted cherry tomatoes and pitta chips for dipping.

1kg (2lb 4oz) squash or butternut squash, cut into wedges

1 whole garlic bulb, cloves separated but left unpeeled

10 sage leaves, plus a few extra to serve

Good pinch of chilli flakes

3 tbsp olive oil

250g (9oz) soft goats' cheese (or vegetarian alternative)

Squeeze of lemon juice

Extra virgin olive oil, for drizzling

75g (3oz) roughly chopped walnut halves or hazelnuts

250g (9oz) pack shop-bought tortellini (such as spinach and ricotta or pumpkin)

25g (1oz) unsalted butter

Drizzle of runny honey

Sea salt and freshly ground black pepper

1   Preheat the oven to 200°C/180°C fan/400°F/Gas 6. Put the squash into a roasting tray with the garlic, sage and chilli flakes. Drizzle with the oil and season well, then toss to combine and roast for 40 minutes, turning once, until golden and slightly sticky. Once cooked, squish the garlic out of their skins and mix into the squash mix.

2   Meanwhile, beat the cheese with the lemon juice and a drizzle of extra virgin olive oil with a whisk or in a small food processor until light, fluffy and smooth. Season well and scoop into a bowl. Toast the nuts and set aside.

3   Cook the tortellini in boiling salted water for 2–3 minutes then drain. Fry the remaining sage leaves in a little olive oil in a frying pan (skillet) until crisp, then scoop onto kitchen paper. Add the butter to the frying pan until it foams and smells nutty, then toss the tortellini in the brown butter.

4   Divide the whipped cheese between four plates. Top with the buttery tortellini, roasted squash and toasted nuts. Drizzle with honey, scatter with sage leaves and serve.

Danish Frikadeller with Charred Cabbage, Gravy & Fresh Egg Tagliatelle

◎ Serves 4

🍶 10 minutes

🍲 30 minutes

Classic Scandi comfort food! Charring cabbage provides a sweet smokiness that works wonderfully with the rich gravy and meatballs here. Serve this with new potatoes or freshly cooked tagliatelle as here.

300g (10oz) minced (ground) veal or beef
300g (10oz) minced (ground) pork
1 banana shallot, finely chopped
2 tbsp fresh breadcrumbs
1 garlic clove, grated
3 sprigs of thyme, leaves stripped
Large handful of finely chopped fresh dill
1 free-range egg
Good grating of fresh nutmeg
1 hispi or pointed cabbage
3 tbsp olive oil
20g (¾oz) unsalted butter
25g (1oz) plain (all-purpose) flour
400ml (1¾ cups) fresh beef or chicken stock
100ml (scant ½ cup) double (heavy) cream
400g (14oz) fresh egg tagliatelle
Sea salt and freshly ground black pepper

1. Preheat the oven to 200°C/180°C fan/400°F/Gas 6.

2. Mix the minced meats with the shallot, breadcrumbs, garlic, thyme, half the dill, the egg and nutmeg. Season well and mix together, then shape into 18 balls about the size of a walnut.

3. Heat a large griddle pan over a high heat. Cut the cabbage into wedges and rub all over with half the oil. Season and char on the cut sides on the griddle then transfer to a roasting tray, season well and roast for 15 minutes.

4. Heat the rest of the oil in the pan and brown the meatballs all over. Transfer to a plate. Add the butter to the fat in the pan, then add the flour and cook for a minute before gradually stirring in the stock and bubbling for 3–4 minutes until you have a thick gravy. Add the cream and then return the meatballs to the pan and simmer while you cook the pasta.

5. Cook the pasta in boiling salted water for 3–4 minutes until tender, then drain and divide between four bowls. Top each with a wedge or two of cabbage then spoon over the meatballs and sauce. Scatter with the remaining dill and serve.

Greeneroni Soup & Broccoli Grilled Cheese

◎ Serves 4

□ 10 minutes

□ 20 minutes

(VE) Vegetarian

Soups keep our family kitchen ticking over. They are the solution to urgent cries for lunch and are essentially an IV drip of vegetables to hungry mouths. This one is particularly delicious – think of it as a spring minestrone and use whatever beautiful green vegetables you can cook in the broth – I love to add shards of savoy cabbage. The grilled cheese here is ashamedly pinched from Pinterest but is surprisingly delicious and adds a layer of green to a sandwich not usually known for its virtuosity.

1   Heat the oil in a large pan and gently fry the spring onions, celery, garlic and courgette for 10 minutes. Add the stock, season well and bring to the boil. Add the pasta and cook for 10 minutes, then add the peas and cook for a few minutes more.

2   Meanwhile, preheat the oven to 200°C/180°C/400°F/Gas 6. Toss the broccoli with the chives and season well. Mix the two cheeses together. Place an ovenproof frying pan or griddle pan over a high heat. Butter the outside of your bread slices and spread the inside with the mustard. Layer up the slices with broccoli, cheese and then broccoli, then top with a second slice.

3   Put the sandwiches in the hot pan and press down firmly with a spatula. Cook until golden on one side then flip and transfer the pan to the oven for 5 minutes until melted and golden. Cut in half and serve with the soup.

2 tbsp olive oil
6 spring onions (scallions), thinly sliced
4 celery sticks, thinly sliced
2 garlic cloves, thinly sliced
1 large courgette (zucchini), diced
1 litre (4 cups) fresh veg stock
150g (5oz) small pasta
150g (5oz) frozen garden peas
Sea salt and freshly ground black pepper

For the grilled cheese

100g (3½oz) broccoli, finely chopped
Small handful of chives, finely chopped
75g (3oz) Cheddar cheese (or vegetarian alternative), grated
85g (3¼oz) Gruyère cheese (or vegetarian alternative), grated
8 slices of white sourdough
30g (1oz) butter, softened
2 tsp Dijon mustard

Fennel and Herb-roasted Pork Belly Feast

◎ Serves 6

🍶 15 minutes

🍲 1½ hours

I grew up with the tradition of a Sunday roast dinner with the whole family and while my mum's classic was a roast chicken (see page 156), I do love pork. I cooked this for a celebration dinner when we moved to Ireland. This pork belly slow-roasted with rosemary and fennel seeds yields incredibly tender meat with crispy crackling. If you don't manage to get the skin as crisp as you like, simply remove the skin from the cooked pork and return to the oven until crispy. This recipe works very well with pork shoulder if you prefer a less fatty cut.

750g (1lb 10oz) new baby potatoes
1.5kg (3lb 5oz) boned and rolled pork belly (with skin)
2 red onions, cut into wedges
2 tbsp fennel seeds
3 sprigs of rosemary
Finely grated zest of 1 lemon, plus a squeeze of juice
1 whole garlic bulb, cloves separated
4 tbsp olive oil
2 bunches of spring onions (scallions), trimmed
2 little gem lettuces, leaves separated and sliced into thin quarters
50g (2oz) wild rocket (arugula)
1 tbsp red wine vinegar
Pinch of sugar
3 tbsp extra virgin olive oil
Sea salt and freshly ground black pepper

1   Preheat the oven to 220°C/200°C fan/425°F/Gas 7. Put the potatoes into a pan of cold salted water, bring to the boil, then simmer for 15 minutes until tender. Drain and tip into a large roasting tray and crush a little with a fork.

2   Put the pork into the same roasting tray with the red onions. Scatter with the fennel seeds and add the rosemary sprigs, lemon zest and garlic cloves. Drizzle all over with most of the oil and season really well with flaky sea salt.

3   Roast for 30 minutes, then reduce the heat to 160°C/140°C fan/325°F/Gas 3 and roast for a further 45 minutes or until the crackling is crisp and the meat tender. (You can check the internal cooking temperature using a meat thermometer – 70°C/160°F is what you should be aiming for.) Allow to rest for 15 minutes. If the potatoes need a little more crisping you can leave them in the oven, increasing the heat back up to 200°C/180°C fan/400°F/Gas 6, for 15 minutes more.

4   Rub the spring onions with the remaining oil. Heat a griddle pan to high and char them for a minute or two, then season and keep warm. Put the little gem and rocket in a bowl, then whisk together the vinegar, sugar, plenty of seasoning and the extra virgin olive oil and pour over the leaves.

5   Slice the pork and serve with the crispy spuds, griddled spring onions, the garlic cloves squeezed from their skins and salad with the resting juices and onions from the tin.

Kale, Ricotta, Potato & Pesto Bake

◎ Serves 6

⏱ 10 minutes

🍲 50 minutes

Ⓥ Vegetarian

Potato bakes are the ultimate in warmth and comfort and using pesto instead of a classic double (heavy) cream and cheese mixture makes this a fabulous light version that's great for a midweek supper or weekend comfort.

200g (7oz) curly kale
1kg (2lb 4oz) floury potatoes, peeled and thickly sliced
300g (10oz) soft ricotta cheese (or vegetarian alternative)
120ml (½ cup) vegetable stock
75g (3oz) mozzarella, grated

For the pesto
50g (2oz) fresh basil
30g (1oz) flat-leaf parsley
2 garlic cloves
50g (2oz) Parmesan cheese (or vegetarian alternative)
30g (1oz) toasted pine nuts
5 tbsp extra virgin olive oil
Sea salt and freshly ground black pepper

1   Make the pesto. Blitz the herbs and garlic together then whizz in the Parmesan and pine nuts. Gradually add the oil (with the motor still running) until you have a luscious pesto. Add a splash of water if it is too thick (you want it to slide off the spoon in an easy dollop). Season and set aside.

2   Preheat the oven to 200°C/180°C fan/400°F/Gas 6.

3   Blanch the kale in boiling water for 2 minutes, then drain, squeeze out any extra water and roughly chop.

4   Put the potatoes into a pan of cold salted water, bring to the boil then simmer for 2–3 minutes and drain.

5   Mix the ricotta with the pesto and the vegetable stock. Mix the kale and potatoes together and tip into a baking dish then pour over the creamy pesto and stir through. Scatter with the mozzarella.

6   Bake for 50 minutes until golden and bubbling. Leave to stand for 5 minutes before serving .

Spicy Prawn Aglio e Olio

◎ Serves 4

▯ 10 minutes

▭ 10 minutes

One of the most popular recipes on my YouTube channel is Spaghetti Aglio e Olio. A slick of oily sautéed garlic forms the sauce and like many of the classic pasta recipes, it is its simplicity that makes it so attractive and rewarding to make. Here it's made all the more crave-worthy with the addition of plump prawns and a shot of spice in the form of chilli flakes. If you have fresh chilli, slice thinly and add as optional extra heat.

500g (1lb 2oz) raw king prawns (jumbo shrimp), shelled and deveined

4–5 tbsp olive oil

6 garlic cloves, thinly sliced

Finely grated zest and juice of 1 lemon

400g (14oz) spaghetti

1 tsp chilli flakes

4 anchovies in oil

Sea salt and freshly ground black pepper

Handful of fresh basil leaves, to garnish

1   Put the prawns into a bowl with tablespoon of the olive oil, a quarter of the sliced garlic and the lemon zest and leave to marinate for 5–10 minutes.

2   Bring a large pan of salted water to the boil and cook the spaghetti for 8–10 minutes until al dente.

3   Meanwhile, heat the remaining oil in a large frying pan over a medium heat, add the remaining garlic, the chilli flakes and anchovies. Cook gently, stirring regularly until the garlic sizzles and turns lightly golden and the anchovies have dissolved.

4   Add the prawns and the marinade, increase the heat and cook for 2–3 minutes, turning halfway, until they are pink all over. Once cooked, add the lemon juice and toss through.

5   Using tongs, scoop the cooked spaghetti directly from its cooking water into the frying pan and toss to coat in all the lemony pan juices, stirring vigorously until completely combined. If necessary, add some of the pasta water to loosen the sauce. Season generously with salt and pepper, scatter with the basil leaves and serve immediately.

Mum's Roast Chicken Dinner

⊚ Serves 4–6

⬡ 30 minutes

⬠ 1¼ hours

Growing up, the Sunday roast was an important part of the weekly routine – it was the ceremonious ending to a weekend well spent, and made way for the week ahead. By Sunday mid-morning, my mum would bang away in the kitchen, no matter what the madness of the week threw, she always pulled it out of the bag, and this was no small feat. She continued this labour of love well into our teens; even when we decided we had far more important things to do, there would always be a plate with the best bits of the meal sitting on the kitchen counter awaiting our late arrival. The unspoken love in families is often seen through these small but memorable actions that stay with us. This is her classic roast. To get a crispy skin, pat the chicken dry before putting the butter under and on top of the skin.

10 garlic cloves, peeled
4 sprigs of thyme, leaves picked
100g (3½oz) butter, softened
1 free-range chicken (about 1.6kg/3lb 8oz)
Sea salt and freshly ground black pepper

For the potatoes

1.5kg (3lb 5oz) floury potatoes, peeled and quartered if large
5 tbsp rapeseed oil

For the carrots and peas

500g (1lb 2oz) carrots, cut into 2cm (¾in) diagonal slices
50g (2oz) butter
100ml (3½fl oz) water
2 tsp sugar
200g (7oz) frozen peas, defrosted
Small handful of chopped flat-leaf parsley

For the gravy

20g (¾oz) plain (all-purpose) flour
125ml (½ cup) white wine
250ml (1 cup) chicken stock

1   Preheat the oven to 200°C/180°C fan/400°F/Gas 6.

2   Put the potatoes into a pan of cold salted water, bring to the boil and simmer for 5 minutes. Drain then return to the pan over a low heat and toss to fluff up and dry the spuds.

3   Meanwhile, add the garlic, thyme and a generous pinch of sea salt to a large pestle and mortar. Bash to a smooth paste before adding the butter and gently mash to combine. Ease the chicken skin away from the flesh using your fingers. Push most of the butter under the skin and spread the rest on top to coat the breast. Put the chicken into a roasting tin.

4   Tip the par-boiled potatoes into another large roasting tin, drizzle with the oil and toss together. Put on the bottom shelf of the oven and put the chicken on the shelf above. Toss the potatoes every so often as they cook.

5   Roast for 50 minutes–an hour until the chicken is fully cooked, golden and the juices run clear when a skewer is inserted into the thickest part of the thigh. Remove from the oven and transfer to a warm plate to rest, then increase the oven temperature to 220°C/200°C fan/425°F/Gas 7 and roast the potatoes for a further 15 minutes.

6   While the chicken and spuds cook, put the carrots, half the butter, the water and sugar into a heavy-based pan along with

some salt and pepper. Cover and simmer for 10–12 minutes until the carrots are tender – they should be coated in a lovely buttery sauce. Add the remaining butter, peas and parsley and toss together until the peas are warm.

7   While the chicken rests, make the gravy. Tilt the pan so the juices run to one end and put the flour in one of the top corners, then gradually whisk in the juices a little at a time until smooth. Place over a medium heat and bubble for 2–3 minutes to cook the flour, then add the wine and bubble for a minute more. Add the stock and bring to the boil, then season to taste and simmer until slightly thickened. Serve with the chicken, spuds and sticky carrots.

⑤ MAKE &

FREEZE

Chicken Inasal Filipino

◎ Serves 4

⌂ 30 minutes, plus infusing and marinating

▢ 50 minutes

✳ Freezer Friendly

A killer grilled chicken from the Philippines which is particularly delicious cooked over hot coals, though a griddle pan in the kitchen will provide the deep smoky char marks required to bring the aromatic marinade to life. The achiote seeds for the oil can easily be found online but you could also replace them with 2 teaspoons of ground turmeric, 1 tablespoon of sweet paprika and the zest of a lime.

1 lemongrass stalk, finely chopped
3cm (1¼in) piece of fresh ginger, peeled and grated
2 garlic cloves, grated
125ml (½ cup) black rice vinegar
1 heaped tbsp soft light brown sugar
Juice of 1 lime
Juice of ½ lemon
75ml (⅓ cup) achiote oil
4 free-range chicken legs
40g (1½oz) unsalted butter
Sea salt and freshly ground black pepper

For the achiote oil

300ml (1¼ cups) neutral oil
100g (3½oz) achiote seeds
2 lemongrass stalks, bashed
4 garlic cloves, bashed
5cm (2in) piece of fresh ginger, sliced

To serve

50ml (2fl oz) rice wine vinegar
50ml (2fl oz) soy sauce
1 green finger chilli, finely chopped
Steamed rice
Small handful of coriander (cilantro) leaves

1   First make the achiote oil. Put all the ingredients into a small pan and simmer very gently for 30 minutes until deep red. Set aside to infuse for at least half an hour, then strain. This will keep in an airtight jar in the fridge for several weeks.

2   For the marinade, mix everything together except the chicken, butter and seasoning. Pour two-thirds into a sealable bag (keep the rest). Make deep incisions into the chicken legs then put them into the bag with the marinade. Leave in the fridge for a few hours, or overnight. Remove from the fridge 30 minutes before cooking.

3   Preheat the oven to 200°C/180°C fan/400°F/Gas 6. Put the rest of the marinade into a small pan with the butter, season well and warm together.

4   Place a heavy-based ovenproof frying pan (skillet) over a high heat and sear the chicken for 5 minutes on each side until there are char marks on both sides. (Alternatively cook on a barbecue.)

5   Baste the legs with the buttery marinade and then transfer to the oven to cook for 20 minutes, basting regularly, until cooked through and glazed.

6   Blend the vinegar, soy and chilli together. Serve the chicken with steamed rice and scatter with coriander leaves, then drizzle with the vinegar, soy and chilli. Add an extra drizzle of the achiote oil, if you like.

How to freeze

Allow the chicken to cool completely, then transfer to freezer bags
with any juices and marinade and freeze for up to 3 months. Defrost
fully then reheat with its juices in a hot oven until piping hot.

Smoky Fish Pie with Velvet Mash Topping

◎ Serves 4

🏺 25 minutes

🍲 45–55 minutes

❄ Freezer Friendly

When it comes to comfort food, having grown up in an Irish fishing village, I have a particular affinity for fish pie. This one is a showstopper. Use a combination of prawns, smoked haddock and a firm white fish like cod for best results. The spinach here is optional, but I always try and sneak in some extra nutrients when I make this for the kids.

1.2kg (2lb 10oz) floury potatoes, cut into chunks
100g (3½oz) butter
75g (3oz) plain (all-purpose) flour
450ml (1¾ cups) whole milk
150ml (scant ⅔ cup) double (heavy) cream
2 tsp Dijon mustard
150g (5oz) baby spinach
200g (7oz) peeled Atlantic prawns (shrimp)
400g (14oz) undyed smoked haddock fillet, skinned and cut into large chunks
400g (14oz) firm white fish fillet, skinned and cut into large chunks
1½ tbsp capers, drained
25g (1oz) finely chopped bunch of flat-leaf parsley
30g (1oz) Gruyère or mature Cheddar cheese, grated
Lemon wedges, to serve
Sea salt and freshly ground black pepper

1   Preheat the oven to 200°C/180°C fan/400°F/Gas 6.

2   Put the potatoes into pan, cover with water, bring to the boil and cook for 15–20 minutes until very tender. Drain, then return to the pan over a medium heat for 30 seconds to dry out. Mash with 40g (1½oz) of the butter and season to taste.

3   Melt the remaining butter in a pan, add the flour and cook for a minute or two, stirring. Gradually stir in the milk and cream to form a thick, shiny, sauce. Stir in the mustard and season to taste. Turn off the heat, then stir in the spinach and wilt.

4   Mix the prawns, fish, capers, and parsley in a 1.2 litre (5 cups) ovenproof dish. Pour over the sauce and mix well. Top with the mashed potato, roughing it up with a fork, then scatter over the cheese.

5   Bake for 30–35 minutes until golden and crisp and the filling is piping hot. Serve with lemon wedges.

Kung Pao Chicken & Aubergine

◎ Serves 4–6

🗍 10 minutes

🍲 20 minutes

❄ Freezer Friendly

Kung pao chicken, a classic Szechuan dish, relies on the numbing heat of Sichuan peppercorns, so they are certainly worth tracking down for this recipe. The aubergine (eggplant) is not traditionally used but works well with the tender chicken.

1 tbsp Sichuan peppercorns
2 tbsp cornflour (cornstarch)
8 free-range skinless chicken thigh fillets, diced
2 tbsp Shaoxing rice wine
5 tbsp soy sauce
3 tbsp runny honey
3 tbsp rice wine vinegar
90ml (3fl oz) vegetable oil
2 aubergines (eggplants), cut into chunks
1 red (bell) pepper, deseeded and cut into pieces
3 garlic cloves, thinly sliced
3cm (1¼in) piece of fresh ginger, peeled and grated
Bunch of spring onions (scallions), thinly sliced
1 tsp chilli flakes
Handful of peanuts
Sea salt and freshly ground black pepper
Steamed rice, to serve

1   Toast the Sichuan peppercorns in a dry pan then grind roughly in a pestle and mortar. Mix with the cornflour in a bowl and season well. Toss in the chicken and add the rice wine and 2 tablespoons of the soy sauce. Mix well until it is coated and sticky.

2   Whisk the rest of the soy sauce with the honey and vinegar to make a sauce and set aside.

3   Heat the oil in a large wok or frying pan (skillet) and fry the aubergines over a high heat for 10–12 minutes until they are golden and squishy. Add the red pepper, garlic, ginger and half the spring onions and fry for a few minutes more. Use a slotted spoon to transfer the vegetables to a bowl.

4   Tip away most of the oil in the pan and then return to a medium-high heat. Add the chicken and chilli flakes and fry until golden all over. Return the vegetables to the pan, add the sauce and cook all together for 3–4 minutes until sticky and fragrant.

5   Scatter with peanuts, the remaining spring onions and serve with steamed rice.

How to freeze

Cool completely and freeze in sealed containers for up to 3 months. Defrost fully then reheat in a hot wok until piping hot.

Irish Farmhouse Vegetable Soup with Rosemary Croutons

◎ Serves 6

🍶 10 minutes

🍲 30 minutes

🆅🅴 Vegetarian

❄ Freezer Friendly

This version is as true to the vegetable soup I grew up with, even though it sometimes came from a carton! It's a real bowl of comfort, particularly if you choose to add the seriously good rosemary croutons – they keep well in an airtight container and are also lovely added to a salad for flavour and crunch.

2 tbsp olive oil
25g (1oz) unsalted butter
1 large onion, sliced
2 garlic cloves, sliced
2 celery sticks, thinly sliced
2 leeks, sliced
1 large carrot, peeled and chopped
1 large parsnip, peeled and chopped
400g (14oz) floury potatoes, diced
600ml (2½ cups) vegetable stock
120g (4oz) frozen peas
Good drizzle of double (heavy) cream
Good grating of fresh nutmeg
Sea salt and freshly ground
   black pepper

For the croutons
 2 tbsp olive oil
20g (¾oz) unsalted butter
2 sprigs of rosemary
2–3 slices of white or sourdough
   bread, diced

1   Heat the oil and butter in a large pan. Add the onion, garlic, celery and leeks and cook for 10 minutes until softened down.

2   Add the rest of the veggies and cook for a few minutes more, then pour in the stock. Season well and bring to the boil, then reduce to a simmer and cook gently for 20 minutes until the veggies are all tender, adding the peas for the last few minutes. Spoon out one-third of the veggies with a slotted spoon and set aside.

3   Blitz the rest of the soup with a stick blender until smooth, then remove from the heat. Stir in the reserved whole veggies.

4   To make the croutons, heat the oil and butter with the rosemary sprigs in a large pan. When hot, add the cubes of bread, toss well then cook for 5–6 minutes until golden and crisp on all sides. Season with sea salt.

5   Add the cream to the soup and a good grating of nutmeg and serve with the rosemary croutons.

How to freeze
Allow to cool completely. Once cool, transfer to a sturdy freezer bag or container and freeze for up to 6 months. Defrost slowly in a pan over a low heat.

Make & Freeze

Roast Vegetable Tagine

◎ Serves 6

⏱ 15 minutes

🍲 1 hour

(VE) Vegetarian

✳ Freezer Friendly

This rich tagine, sweetened with apricots and spiced with ras el hanout is ideal to use whatever vegetables you have to hand, although firmer vegetables like squash, carrot and parsnip do hold up better. It's worth seeking out preserved lemons for this dish for the vibrant citrus kick and depth they add to a stew like this.

1   Preheat the oven to 200°C/180°C fan/400°F/Gas 6.

2   Toss the vegetables with 2 tablespoons of the oil in a large roasting tray. Season well and roast for 40 minutes, turning occasionally.

3   Heat the remaining oil in a casserole and gently fry the garlic, spices and preserved lemon for about a minute. Tip in the roasted vegetables, add the stock, tomatoes and apricots and bring to a simmer. Cook gently for 15 minutes.

4   Scatter with coriander and serve with cooked couscous or bulgur wheat.

2 red onions, sliced into wedges
750g (1lb 10oz) winter squash,
   cut into pieces
2 large parsnips, cut into chunks
2 large carrots, cut into chunks
3 tbsp olive oil
4 garlic cloves, grated
2 tsp ras el hanout
1 tsp ground cumin
1 tsp ground coriander
Pinch of saffron strands
2 preserved lemons, flesh
   removed and skin shredded
300ml (1¼ cups) vegetable stock
400g (14oz) tin cherry tomatoes
100g (3½oz) dried apricots
Sea salt and freshly ground
   black pepper

To serve

400g (14oz) tin chickpeas, drained
   and rinsed
Handful of chopped coriander
   (cilantro)
Cooked couscous or bulgur wheat

How to freeze

Allow to cool, then tip into freezerproof containers and freeze for up to 6 months. Defrost fully then add to a pan with the chickpeas and heat through for 10 minutes.

Chicken & Sweetcorn Soup

◎ Serves 4–6

▢ 10 minutes

▢ 25 minutes

✳ Freezer Friendly

There is something about the sweet, aromatic slurpiness of chicken and sweetcorn soup that brings me instant comfort. The real magic moment of making this is when you swirl beaten egg into the hot liquid to form velvet ribbons that add both sustenance and texture.

1.3 litres (5½ cups) fresh light chicken bone broth or stock
2 large free-range chicken breasts
2cm (¾in) piece of fresh ginger, peeled and thinly sliced into matchsticks
2 garlic cloves, thinly sliced
6 spring onions (scallions), thinly sliced
2 tbsp light soy sauce
3 sweetcorn cobs, kernels removed with a sharp knife (or use 800g/1lb ¾oz tinned or frozen)
1 tbsp cornflour (cornstarch)
2 medium free-range eggs, beaten
Sea salt and freshly ground black pepper

1   Put the chicken stock into a large pan and add the chicken breasts, ginger, garlic and half the spring onions. Bring to the boil then simmer gently for 15–20 minutes until the chicken is cooked through.

2   Remove the chicken with a slotted spoon and when cool enough to handle, shred into pieces.

3   Add the soy sauce and sweetcorn to the stock and simmer for 1–2 minutes. Mix the cornflour with a little of the soup until it is smooth then add this to the pan and cook until the soup is slightly thickened. Return the shredded chicken to the pan.

4   Slowly pour in the eggs while you stir the soup, letting it cook in thin strands. Check the seasoning, add the rest of the spring onions and serve.

How to freeze

Allow the soup to cook completely, then pour into sturdy freezer bags or containers and freeze for up to 3 months. Defrost slowly in a pan over a low heat, then bring to the boil for a minute before serving.

Spicy Peanut Butter Satay Pork

◎ Serves 4

⬚ 10 minutes

⬚ 30 minutes

✳ Freezer Friendly

A rich and creamy satay that relies on one of my favourite pantry ingredients, peanut butter. This also works incredibly well with chicken thigh meat. If you can't find kecap manis, replace with 1 tablespoon dark soy sauce and a little brown sugar to taste.

2 tbsp groundnut (peanut) or vegetable oil
1 onion, thinly sliced
3 garlic cloves, thinly sliced
3cm (1in) piece of fresh ginger, peeled and grated
1 red chilli, deseeded and thinly sliced
500g (1lb 2oz) pork loin fillet, diced
4 tbsp crunchy peanut butter
1 tbsp kecap manis
2 tbsp soy sauce
2 tsp fish sauce
400ml (1¾ cups) tin coconut milk
200g (7oz) baby spinach

To serve

Rice noodles
Juice of 1 lime
Handful of peanuts, chopped
Smalll handful of coriander (cilantro) leaves

1   Heat the oil in a pan over a high heat and fry the onion for 6 minutes until it begins to soften and colour. Add the garlic, ginger and chilli and fry for a couple more minutes until aromatic.

2   Add the diced pork and increase the heat to brown all over, then add the peanut butter, kecap manis, soy sauce, fish sauce and coconut milk.

3   Bring to the boil then reduce the heat and simmer gently for 20 minutes until the pork is tender and the sauce a little reduced and thickened. Add the spinach, remove from the heat and stir until the spinach has wilted.

4   Serve with noodles, squeeze lime juice over the top and sprinkle with peanuts and coriander leaves.

How to freeze

Allow to cool completely, then tip into freezerproof containers and freeze for up to 3 months. Defrost fully, then reheat in a pan until piping hot.

Vegetable Massaman Curry

◎ Serves 4–6

🍶 10 minutes

🍲 40 minutes

❄ Freezer Friendly

A mild yet aromatic curry from Thailand that works wonderfully with chicken and beef; here tofu bulks it out with potatoes, cauliflower and green beans. The texture of tofu changes when you freeze it, becoming almost spongey, but don't worry; this makes it even more delicious as it soaks up the wonderful sauce and all its flavours even better.

3 tbsp vegetable oil
225g (8oz) firm tofu, cut into large dice
2 red onions, thinly sliced
3cm (1¼in) piece of fresh ginger, peeled and grated
3 garlic cloves, grated
1 lemongrass stalk, bashed
3 tbsp massaman curry paste
400g (14oz) sweet potato, peeled and cut into 2cm (¾in) pieces
1 medium (about 500g/1lb 2oz) cauliflower, broken into large florets
2 × 400ml (1¾ cups) tins coconut milk
1 tbsp fish sauce
2 tsp soy sauce
150g (5oz) green beans, trimmed and halved
Sea salt and freshly ground black pepper

To serve

Juice of 1 lime
Handful of coriander (cilantro) leaves
Handful of chopped toasted peanuts
Steamed rice or rice noodles

1   Heat 2 tablespoons of the vegetable oil in a large wok or frying pan (skillet). Fry the tofu until golden all over, then remove and set aside. Add the rest of the oil to the pan and fry the onion, ginger, garlic and lemongrass for 5 minutes until the onion is softened. Add the curry paste and fry for a minute or two.

2   Add the sweet potato and fry for 5 minutes before adding the cauliflower and frying for 2–3 minutes more. Pour in the coconut milk, season well and bring to a simmer. Simmer for 20 minutes, or until the sauce has thickened and the veg has cooked. Add the fried tofu, fish sauce, soy sauce and green beans for the last few minutes.

3   Serve with a good squeeze of lime juice, some coriander leaves and toasted chopped peanuts, and steamed rice or rice noodles.

How to freeze

Allow to cool completely, then transfer to a freezerproof container and freeze for up to 6 months. Defrost fully then reheat over a medium heat until piping hot.

Veggie Marmite & Cheddar Burgers

◎ Serves 6

⧖ 10 minutes, plus resting

▭ 15 minutes

Ⓥ Vegetarian

✳ Freezer Friendly

If you're looking for a really good veggie burger, look no further – this Marmite and Cheddar-infused bean mix holds its shape really well and feels really indulgent sandwiched between brioche buns. Serve with roast sweet potato fries or dressed salad leaves.

1   Blitz the beans in a food processor, then tip into a bowl with the rest of the ingredients apart from the olive oil. Season well and use your hands to mush and squish together.

2   Leave the mixture to rest for 30 minutes in the fridge to soak up moisture and allow the flavours to develop, then shape into 6 patties.

3   Preheat the oven to 200°C/180°C fan/400°F/Gas 6. Heat the oil in a large non-stick pan over a high heat and fry the burgers for 2–3 minutes on each side, until they are crispy and golden on the outside.

4   Transfer the burgers to a baking sheet and top each with a slice of cheese. Cook for 10 minutes until the cheese has melted and the burger is hot through.

5   Serve the burgers in toasted brioche buns with a dollop of mayonnaise, sliced tomatoes and sliced avocado.

400g (14oz) tin kidney beans, drained and rinsed
400g (14oz) tin cannellini beans, drained and rinsed
2 tsp Marmite
1 medium free-range egg
2 tsp Dijon mustard
2 tsp black treacle
3 tbsp flat-leaf parsley
75g (3oz) fresh brown breadcrumbs
75g (3oz) Cheddar cheese (or vegetarian alternative), grated
2 tbsp olive oil
Sea salt and freshly ground black pepper

To serve

6 slices of Cheddar cheese (or vegetarian alternative)
6 brioche buns, lightly toasted
6 dollops of mayonnaise
3 large ripe tomatoes, sliced
2 ripe avocados, sliced

How to freeze

Layer the shaped patties up between sheets of baking parchment and wrap well in parchment and foil. Freeze for up to 6 months. Defrost fully before cooking.

Minestrone with Parmesan & Pesto

◎ Serves 6

🖐 10 minutes

🍲 30 minutes

Ⓥ Vegetarian

✳ Freezer Friendly

There are soups that I revisit regularly and this one is a firm favourite in our house. It's straightforward to prepare and yields a big pot that will feed the whole family. Try to seek out tinned cherry tomatoes for this – they add a unique sweetness.

3 tbsp olive oil
1 large onion, finely chopped
2 celery sticks, finely chopped,
  leaves saved and chopped
2 carrots, finely chopped
2 garlic cloves, grated
1 large courgette (zucchini),
  chopped
200g (7oz) frozen peas
  or broad beans
1 large potato (about 250g/9oz),
  peeled and diced
400g (14oz) tin cherry tomatoes
750ml (3 cups) vegetable stock
  (or use chicken stock)
Sea salt and freshly ground
  black pepper

To serve

400g (14oz) tin white beans
200g (7oz) baby spinach
50g (2oz) Parmesan cheese
  (or vegetarian equivalent), grated
6 tbsp fresh basil pesto
  (see page 152)

1   Heat the oil in a large pan and gently fry the onion, celery, carrot and garlic for 10 minutes. Add the rest of the ingredients, and stir together and season well. Bring to a simmer and cook for 15–20 minutes.

2   Add the white beans and spinach and simmer for 3–4 minutes. Serve with grated Parmesan and a dollop of fresh basil pesto.

How to freeze

Cool the soup completely and then freeze in sturdy bags or a freezerproof container. Defrost slowly in a pan and bring to a simmer.

Chicken Noodle Soup

◎ Serves 6

🍶 10 minutes

🍲 1½ hours

❄ Freezer Friendly

This is based on the classic Jewish chicken soup, a wonderful cure-all that nourishes the soul. Parsley root has a delicious fragrant flavour and is well worth hunting down if you can, but parsnip works well as an alternative.

1 free-range chicken (about 1.8kg/4lb)
8 black peppercorns
6 garlic cloves, unpeeled
Small bunch of flat-leaf parsley
2 white onions, sliced
2 carrots, peeled and sliced
2 celery sticks, thinly sliced
2 parsley roots (or 1 parsnip), peeled and sliced
Small bunch of dill
300g (10oz) small pasta or crushed spaghetti
Sea salt

1 Put the chicken in a large stockpot or casserole. Add the peppercorns and garlic cloves and the stalks of the parsley. Add a generous amount of flaky sea salt and then cover with 1.2 litres (5 cups) of cold water (or enough to just cover the chicken) and bring to the boil. Skim off any scum that floats to the surface then reduce to a simmer and gently bubble, covered, for 45 minutes.

2 Add the vegetables and dill and simmer for a further 15 minutes. Remove the chicken and veggies from the pan with a slotted spoon. Bring the soup up to the boil and bubble, uncovered, for 15 minutes to intensify the flavour. Allow to cool completely.

3 Shred the meat from the bones of the chicken and return to the soup with the veggies.

4 Add the pasta to the soup and simmer gently until al dente then serve in large bowls.

How to freeze

Allow to cool, then transfer to a ziplock bag or freezerproof container and freeze for up to 3 months. Warm slowly in a pan to defrost.

Make & Freeze

Chickpea, Tomato & Lentil Soup with Spiced Oil

◎ Serves 4

▯ 10 minutes, plus infusing

▭ 40 minutes

Ⓥ Vegan

✳ Freezer Friendly

As my grandad would say, this is a soup with eatin' and drinkin' in it! A hearty bowl made with staple ingredients and kicked up a notch with a stellar spiced oil that provides the soup with a finishing touch of aromatic heat. The oil can be stored in a jar in the fridge for about a month and used to drizzle over cooked meat, to dip bread into or to pep up soups and stews like this.

1   Heat the oil in a pan and gently fry the onion and garlic for 10 minutes until soft. Add the spices and fry for a few minutes before adding the tomatoes and plenty of seasoning. Allow them to cook down for 3-4 minutes.

2   Pour in the stock, bring to a simmer and cook for 15 minutes, then add the lentils and chickpeas and cook for 10 minutes more.

3   Meanwhile, make the spiced oil. Gently heat the oil and spices in a pan over a low heat and then remove from the heat and leave to infuse for at least 10 minutes.

4   Serve the warm soup with crusty bread, a drizzle of the spiced oil and a scattering of parsley leaves.

2 tbsp olive oil
1 large onion, finely chopped
2 garlic cloves, grated
1 tsp ground cumin
½ tsp ground turmeric
400g (14oz) fresh tomatoes, chopped
600ml (2½ cups) vegetable stock
250g (9oz) pack ready-cooked green or puy lentils
400g (14oz) tin chickpeas, drained and rinsed
Sea salt and freshly ground black pepper

For the spiced oil

75ml (⅓ cup) olive oil
1 tsp cumin seeds
1 tsp coriander seeds
Good pinch of chilli flakes

To serve

Crusty bread
Handful of flat-leaf parsley leaves

How to freeze

Allow to cool, then transfer to a sturdy freezer bag or container and freeze for up to 6 months. Defrost slowly in a pan over a low heat.

⑥ FAVOURITE DESSERTS

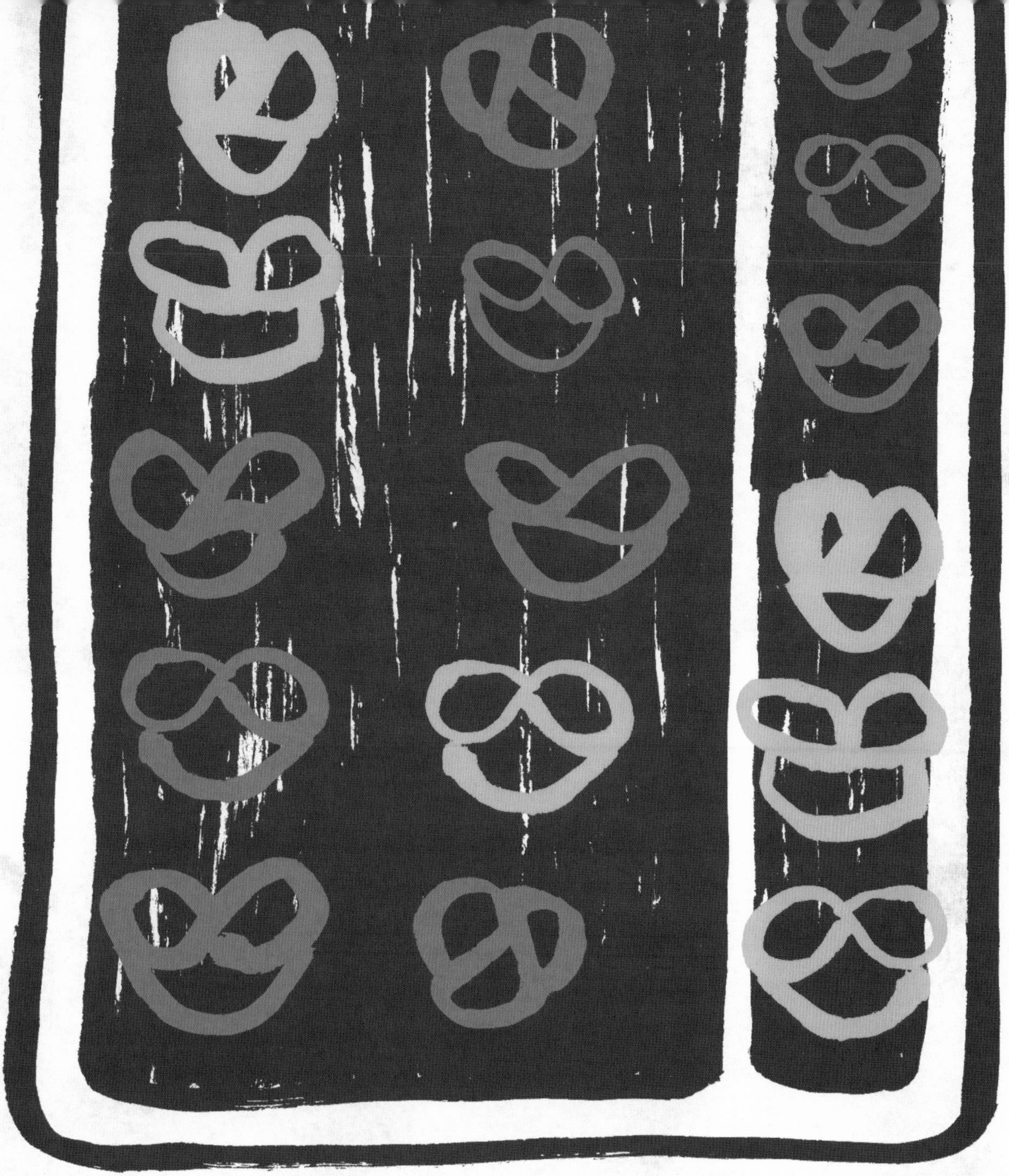

Sticky Toffee Pudding

◎ Serves 6

⏱ 20 minutes

▭ 45 minutes

One of my desert island desserts will forever be sticky toffee pud, but in our busy family kitchen the thought of preparing dariole moulds and then trying to coax the cooked mini puddings out is anxiety-inducing. This version, while you might think me lazy, works a treat as the date-laden treacly batter is baked in one big baking dish and served straight to the table with a cheat's salted toffee sauce and a tub of shop-bought vanilla ice cream. The toffee sauce can be made in advance and will keep in a jar in the fridge for up to 2 weeks.

150g (5oz) salted butter, softened,
    plus extra for greasing
175g (6oz) light muscovado sugar
1 tbsp golden syrup
2 tbsp black treacle
2 large free-range eggs
1 tsp vanilla extract
200g (1½ cups) self-raising flour
300ml (1¼ cups) water
175g (6oz) chopped dried dates
1 tbsp bicarbonate soda
    (baking soda)
Tub of vanilla ice cream, to serve

For the toffee sauce
100g (3½oz) salted butter
150g (5oz) dark muscovado sugar
3 tbsp golden syrup
150ml (scant ⅔ cup) double
    (heavy) cream
1 tsp vanilla extract

1   Preheat the oven to 200°C/180°C fan/400°F/Gas 6 and lightly butter a 20cm (8in) round ovenproof dish.

2   Blend the butter and muscovado sugar together in a food mixer on high speed. Add the golden syrup, treacle, eggs and vanilla and continue to mix. When combined turn the mixer to slow speed and add the flour and mix until fully combined.

3   Put the water and dates into a pan and bring to the boil. After it has boiled for a few minutes add the bicarbonate of soda – be careful as the mixture will foam up – then add this bubbly date mixture to the cake mixture while it is still hot. Combine the two and then pour into the prepared cake tin. Bake for 45 minutes, or until firm and slightly springy to the touch.

4   Meanwhile, make the toffee sauce. Melt the butter, sugar and golden syrup together in a small pan until the sugar has dissolved. Add the cream and vanilla extract and bring to a steady simmer for 3 minutes until the toffee sauce has nicely thickened. Remove from the heat.

5   Drizzle the sticky toffee sauce all over the pudding and serve with vanilla ice cream.

Crunchie Banoffee Pie

Serves 6–8

20 minutes, plus chilling

One of the recipes I am most known for is this crunchie banoffee pie from my early days food blogging. Looking back over the past nine cookbooks I was surprised to find it hasn't ever been printed! Without further ado, I present to you a family classic that is, of course, one of the easiest desserts you will ever make but one which will become the most requested.

300g (10oz) dark chocolate digestive biscuits (graham crackers), finely crushed

115g (4oz) salted butter, melted

250ml (1 cup) double (heavy) cream

297g (10oz) tin caramel condensed milk

3 just ripe bananas

3 × 40g (1½oz) Crunchie bars (chocolate-covered honeycomb), roughly chopped

1   Grease and line an 18cm (7in) round loose springform or loose-bottomed cake tin.

2   Mix together the crushed biscuits with the melted butter until they are combined and then press the mixture evenly over the base of the cake tin. Leave to set in the fridge for about 2 hours until firm. When the base is ready, carefully remove it from the tin and place on a cake stand or plate.

3   Pour the cream into a bowl and whisk until soft peaks form. Carefully spread the caramel evenly over the biscuit base.

4   Slice the bananas evenly and place on top of the layer of caramel. Now add the cream on top of the banana and to finish it off, sprinkle the Crunchie bars over the top of the cream as artistically as you feel necessary. Cover and chill until you are ready to serve.

Chocolate Biscuit Cake

◎ Serves 8

⌷ 20 minutes, plus
chilling

Forever a classic and a staple at children's birthday parties, chocolate biscuit cake is worth revisiting for the nostalgia alone. This version has a chocolate glaze that gives it a glossy finish with chocolate dripping down the sides to make it look a little more fancy. Once you have melted the butter, golden syrup and chocolate to create a delectable goo feel free to add elements like dried cherries, nuts or broken up chocolate bars to make this your own.

275g (9¾oz) salted butter
150ml (scant ⅔ cup) golden syrup
225g (8oz) good-quality dark chocolate (at least 60% cocoa solids), broken into pieces
200g (7oz) digestive biscuits (graham crackers), roughly crushed
200g (7oz) rich tea biscuits, roughly crushed
50g (2oz) Maltesers
50g (2oz) mini marshmallows

For the glaze

100g (3½oz) good-quality dark chocolate (at least 60% cocoa solids)
30g (1oz) salted butter
50g (2oz) icing (confectioner's) sugar, sifted
75ml (⅓ cup) double (heavy) cream
Hundreds and thousands, to decorate (optional)

1   Grease and line a 15cm (6in) round springform or loose-bottomed cake tin.

2   Melt the butter, syrup and chocolate in a pan over a low heat. Stir to make sure all the ingredients are well mixed together.

3   Add both biscuits, the Maltesers and marshmallows and stir well, then spoon into the prepared tin. Level it on top and press down well to avoid air bubbles. Cover and leave in the fridge for at least 4 hours until solid and set.

4   To make the glaze, melt the chocolate and butter in a small pan. When melted, remove from the heat and whisk in the icing sugar and cream. Allow to cool until the mixture becomes thick enough to leave a figure of eight on the surface. Pour over the cake and sprinkle with hundreds and thousands, if you like. Leave to set at room temperature before cutting.

USE WHAT IS IN YOUR CUPBOARD AND FRIDGE AND DON'T GET HUNG UP ON RECIPES THAT CALL FOR INGREDIENTS YOU DON'T HAVE.

Rice Krispie Treats

◎ **Makes 9–12 squares**

🕐 **20 minutes, plus chilling**

Birthdays and special occasions would not be the same without a sweet treat like these being passed around. A simple but ever popular recipe that can be adapted with toppings of your choice. The pretzels add salty crunch here and are a welcome addition!

4 Snickers bars
2 × 41g (1½oz) tubes of Rolos
150g (5oz) unsalted butter
125g (4oz) Rice Krispies
250g (9oz) milk chocolate
100g (3½oz) salted pretzels

1   Grease and line a 20cm (8in) square cake or baking tin with baking parchment.

2   Put the Snickers bars, Rolos and butter in a bowl and place over a pan of just simmering water, making sure the base of the bowl doesn't touch the water. Gently stir until it is melted and sticky.

3   Remove the bowl from the heat and add the Rice Krispies; mix until evenly combined. Tip into the prepared tin and press down firmly (I use a potato masher) to form a smooth and compacted layer. Place in the fridge to harden.

4   Gently melt the milk chocolate in a clean bowl set over a pan of just simmering water, then pour evenly over the mixture in the tin. Scatter with the pretzels and return to the fridge for at least an hour before cutting into squares.

My Best Summer Pavlova

⊚ Serves 8

🍶 30 minutes

🍲 1½ hours, plus
cooling

It's best to make the meringue for this pavlova the day before so that it has time to cool fully in the oven once you turn it off. Any quick change of temperature will cause the meringue to crack and although a few cracks are normal, especially when the meringue is as mallowy as this, you want to keep the shell as intact as possible before you fill it.

6 large free-range egg whites
360g (13oz) caster (superfine) sugar
1 tsp lemon juice
2 tsp cornflour (cornstarch)

For the filling

225ml (scant 1 cup) rosé wine
150g (5oz) caster (superfine) sugar
1 vanilla pod, split and seeds
  scraped out
Squeeze of lemon juice
3 sprigs of thyme, leaves stripped
4 ripe peaches
250ml (1 cup) double (heavy) cream
150g (5oz) raspberries

1 Preheat the oven to 150°C/130°C fan/300°F/Gas 2. Line a baking sheet with baking parchment and draw a 20cm (8in) circle on it.

2 In a large, clean bowl, whisk the egg whites until they are just holding their shape. Gradually whisk in the sugar, a little at a time, making sure it is dissolved before the next batch, until you have a thick and glossy meringue. Whisk in the lemon juice and cornflour.

3 Dollop all the mixture in a pile in the centre of the drawn circle. Gently spread out to fill the circle, as if you were icing a cake, keeping it nice and high, then smooth around the outside with a spatula. Using a dessert spoon, make an indentation in the centre of the mixture, pushing it gently to the edges. Then with the back of the spoon, go around the outside of the pavlova and drag the spoon up at an angle and slightly tilted inwards to form deep furrows around the circumference.

4 Bake for 20 minutes, then turn down the oven to 110°C/90°C fan/225°F/Gas ¼ and cook for a further 1–1½ hours until the shell is nice and crisp. Turn the oven off but leave the pavlova inside to cool completely.

5 Meanwhile, make the syrup. Put the wine, sugar and vanilla pod and seeds into a pan with a good squeeze of lemon juice and the thyme leaves. Place over a low heat and gently melt the sugar, then increase the heat and bubble until it is lightly syrupy and coats the back of a spoon.

6   Meanwhile, bring a pan of water to the boil. Make a small cross in the bottom of each peach then drop them into the water for 20 seconds. Remove and plunge into a bowl of cold water. Carefully peel and halve them and remove the stones and slice. Pour the warm rosé syrup over the peaches (discard the vanilla pod) and set aside to cool.

7   When you are ready to serve, lightly whip the cream. Put the pavlova on a serving plate and pile the cream in the centre. Top with the peaches and syrup and scatter with raspberries.

Auntie Ann's Chocolate Chip Banana Bread

◎ Serves 8

◻ 20 minutes

◻ 50 minutes

Another classic recipe in our house is my Auntie Ann's famous chocolate chip banana bread. It's an old recipe she picked up from her time spent in Cape Breton Island in Nova Scotia, Canada and has been made countless times in our house. More cake than bread, it's sweet and moist due to the combination of caster sugar, light brown sugar and three very ripe bananas. Nuts are optional!

110g (4oz) salted butter, softened, plus extra for greasing
240g (scant 2 cups) self-raising flour, plus extra for dusting
100g (3½oz) caster (superfine) sugar
100g (3½oz) soft light brown sugar
2 large free-range eggs
1 tsp baking powder
3 large, very ripe bananas (the browner the better)
½ tsp vanilla extract
50g (2oz) dark chocolate chips
80g (3¼oz) chopped walnuts (optional)
1 small banana, halved lengthways

1 Preheat the oven to 180°C/160°C fan/350°F/Gas 4. Grease a 900g (2lb) loaf tin and dust with flour.

2 Whisk the caster sugar, 90g of the brown sugar and the butter in a bowl with a hand-held electric mixer until light and pale. Add one of the eggs and a little of the flour and mix through, then repeat with the other egg and the rest of flour and baking powder, until everything is mixed through and smooth.

3 Mash the 3 large bananas roughly with the back of a fork (you don't want to make them too smooth). Add them to a bowl with the vanilla extract and mix through, then add the chocolate chips and chopped nuts, if using.

4 Pour the mix into the prepared loaf tin, arrange the halved banana on top, sprinkle with the remaining brown sugar and bake for about 50 minutes, or until a skewer inserted in the centre comes out clean. Check after 25 minutes; if it looks like it's browning too much cover it with some foil. Cool for 10 minutes in the tin before turning out onto a wire rack to cool completely.

Showstopper Butterscotch Puddings

◎ Serves 4
(makes 2 large or 4
small desserts)

🕓 15 minutes, plus
chilling

🍲 15 minutes

The butterscotch puddings at LA's Gjelina restaurant, are said to be the most talked about menu item and for good reason. Sweet little pots of joy in the form of a rich butterscotch with a slick of caramel sauce on top, cut with crème fraîche and a sprinkle of sea salt – it's a dessert I regularly dream of. They're also ideal for entertaining as they can be made at least a day ahead.

1   Melt the butter in a medium heavy-based saucepan. Add the brown sugar and cook for 2–3 minutes, stirring occasionally, until the sugar has dissolved. Add the cream and bring to a simmer, stirring until you have a nice thick butterscotch sauce.

2   Meanwhile, put the cornflour into a bowl with the salt and loosen with a couple of tablespoons of the milk until smooth, then whisk into the rest of the milk in a large bowl. Whisk in the egg yolks with the vanilla extract and then gradually add the hot butterscotch sauce, whisking constantly.

3   Wipe out the butterscotch pan, then strain the mixture back into it through a fine-mesh sieve. Cook over a medium heat for 5–6 minutes, stirring regularly, until the butterscotch custard starts to thicken. Remove from the heat and pour into 2 or 4 pretty glasses or ramekins. Chill for at least 1 hour or up to 3 days.

4   To make the caramel sauce, put the butter, sugar and golden syrup into a pan and bring to a gentle boil, then simmer until the sugar has dissolved. Add the cream, vanilla and salt and whisk together; simmer for 3 minutes until the sauce is thick and sticky. You can use the sauce right away or transfer to a jar and refrigerate when cool to use as needed. The sauce will keep for up to 7 days in the fridge.

5   To serve, drizzle the puddings with caramel sauce, top with a dollop of crème fraîche and add a final drizzle of sauce.

2 tbsp salted butter, softened
75g (3oz) soft dark brown sugar
120ml (½ cup) double (heavy) cream
1 tbsp cornflour (cornstarch)
Pinch of salt
190ml (¾ cup) milk
2 medium free-range egg yolks
½ tsp vanilla extract
125g (4oz) crème fraîche, to serve

For the salted caramel sauce

50g (2oz) butter
75g (3oz) soft dark brown sugar
1 generous tbsp golden syrup
75ml (⅓ cup) double (heavy) cream
½ tsp vanilla extract
Pinch of sea salt

Boozy Brownie Meringue Cake

◎ Serves 8

🍶 20 minutes

🍲 40–45 minutes

A perfect mix of gooey brownie and crisp and chewy meringue. Switch things up by swapping the icing sugar for cocoa powder or by adding chocolate shavings on top. Be sure to take the brownie out while it still has a little wobble, otherwise you will overcook it when it goes back in the oven with the meringue topping.

For the brownie

225g (8oz) salted butter, plus extra for greasing
225g (8oz) good-quality dark chocolate (at least 60% cocoa solids)
300g (10oz) caster (superfine) sugar
3 large free-range eggs, beaten
1 tsp vanilla extract
100g (scant 1 cup) plain (all-purpose) flour
1 tsp baking powder

For the meringue

200g (7oz) icing (confectioner's) sugar, plus extra to serve
3 free-range large egg whites
1 tsp cornflour (cornstarch)
½ tsp white wine vinegar

For the topping

450ml (1¾ cups) double (heavy) cream
50g (2oz) icing (confectioner's) sugar
2 tbsp brandy
30g (1oz) chopped toasted hazelnuts
Gold stars, glitter and indoor sparklers (optional)

1   Preheat the oven to 180°C/160°C fan/350°F/Gas 4 and grease and line a 20cm (8in) round springform cake tin with baking parchment.

2   Put the chocolate and butter into a heatproof bowl and set over a pan of barely simmering water, making sure the base of the bowl doesn't touch the water. Stir constantly until melted and smooth.

3   Put the sugar and eggs into a separate bowl and use a hand-held electric mixer to whisk until pale and fluffy, about 2–3 minutes. Slowly add the melted chocolate and butter, then add the vanilla extract and continue to whisk until thickened. Lastly, sift in the flour and baking powder and fold in gently.

4   Turn the mixture into the prepared tin and bake in the middle of the oven for 20–25 minutes until the top is firm and the cake has come away slightly from the sides of the tin. Keep the oven on for the meringue.

5   Meanwhile, make the meringue. Put the icing sugar and egg whites into the bowl of a stand mixer and whisk on high speed for 10 minutes until glossy white peaks form. Using a spatula, gently fold in the cornflour and the vinegar. Pour the mixture on top of the brownie and bake for another 20 minutes, then remove from the oven and allow to cool completely.

6   Once cooled, carefully remove from the tin and place on a cake stand. Whip the cream with the icing sugar until pillowy but still soft and then fold in the brandy. Dollop onto the top of the cake, then sprinkle with the hazelnuts. Add gold stars, glitter and indoor sparklers for a special occasion and serve.

CONFIDENCE IN THE KITCHEN IS THE BEST *TOOL YOU* CAN ARM YOURSELF WITH.

Key Lime Pretzel Pie

◎ Serves 8–10

⬖ 20 minutes, plus chilling

⬓ 25 minutes

A sharp, sweet key lime pie piled high with whipped cream will forever be one of my hero desserts. It's a showstopping crowd-pleaser that always has people asking for seconds. A wonderful make-ahead dessert that can be revealed to great fanfare at the end of any feast!

For the pretzel crust

250g (9oz) digestive biscuits (graham crackers), finely crushed
25g (1oz) salted pretzels, finely crushed
1 tbsp caster sugar
50g (2oz) butter, melted

For the filling

About 5–6 limes
4 large free-range egg yolks
½ tsp cream of tartar
396g (14oz) tin sweetened condensed milk

For the topping

250ml (1 cup) double (heavy) cream
2 tbsp icing (confectioner's) sugar
125g (4oz) Greek yoghurt
1 tbsp dark rum (optional)

For the candied lime zest

140g (4½ oz) golden caster (superfine) sugar, plus extra for dusting
150ml water (scant ⅔ cup)
Reserved lime zest strips

1　Preheat the oven to 160°C/140°C fan/325°F/Gas 3 and place a 20cm (8in) fluted flan tin on a baking sheet.

2　Combine the digestives, pretzels, sugar and melted butter in a large bowl until it holds together when pressed between your fingers (add more melted butter if too dry).

3　Tip the mixture into the flan tin and press in an even layer across the bottom and up the sides until you have a firm pie crust. Bake for 10 minutes, or until lightly golden and firm to touch. Remove from the oven and allow to cool completely.

4　To make the filling remove the zest from the limes in strips using a zester and set aside for the candied lime zest. Juice the limes into a measuring jug until you have 120ml (½ cup) juice.

5　Whisk the egg yolks in a bowl using a hand-held electric whisk until they are thickened and lighter in colour. Whisk in the cream of tartar and condensed milk on low speed, a little at a time, until combined. Continue to whisk as you pour in the lime juice until incorporated. Pour into the cooled crust.

6　Bake the pie for about 15 minutes, or until the filling has just set around the edges but the centre still has a slight wobble. Remove and allow to cool slightly before transferring to a wire rack to cool completely.

7　While the pie cools, prepare the topping. Whip the cream and icing sugar together in a large bowl until stiff peaks form. Using a spatula, fold through the yoghurt and rum (if using). Place dollops of the cream on top of the cooled pie and create swirls. Chill in the fridge for about 2 hours – if you can wait!

8   Make the candied lime zest. Put the golden caster sugar and
    water into a small pan. Place over a medium heat and bring
    to the boil, then turn down to a simmer. Add the strips of lime
    peel and cook gently for 25 minutes until the peel has softened
    and the syrup has thickened.

9   Dust a sheet of baking parchment with golden caster sugar. Lift
    the softened lime peel out of the pan with a slotted spoon and
    roll in the sugar to coat. Leave to cool until hardened. (This will
    keep in an airtight container for up to a month.)

10 When you are ready to serve, remove the pie from the fridge
    and decorate with the candied lime zest. Enjoy!

Perfect Fudgy Dark & White Ripple Brownies with Raspberries

◎ Makes 16 squares

⏱ 20 minutes

🍲 35–40 minutes

Melting white chocolate can be tricky. When it is in the bowl over a pan of just simmering water, don't stir it or it may well seize and go lumpy – leave it for 10 minutes and even though it won't look melted it will be fine.

100g (3½oz) dark chocolate, broken into pieces
100g (3½oz) white chocolate, broken into pieces
150g (5oz) unsalted butter, softened
200g (7oz) caster (superfine) sugar
75g (3oz) soft light brown sugar
3 large free-range eggs
1 tsp vanilla bean paste
150g (5oz) plain (all-purpose) flour
150g (5oz) raspberries

1   Preheat the oven to 180°C/160°C fan/350°F/Gas 4 and grease and line a 20cm (8in) square cake tin with baking parchment.

2   Melt the dark chocolate in a heatproof bowl set over a pan of just simmering water. Set aside to cool a little bit. Do the same with the white chocolate in a separate bowl.

3   With a hand-held electric whisk, beat the butter and both sugars together until light and fluffy. Beat the eggs together in a small jug then gradually pour them into the butter and sugar mixture, whisking the whole time until you have a fluffy smooth mix. Beat in the vanilla bean paste and then the flour. Divide the mixture in half.

4   Gently fold the melted dark chocolate into one half of the mixture and the white chocolate into the other half.

5   Roughly dollop the mixture like a checker board into the prepared tin and push the raspberries into the mixture. Us the end of a teaspoon to swirl the two colours together.

6   Bake the brownies for 35–40 minutes so that a skewer comes out almost clean but still a little bit sticky. Leave to cool completely in the tin before cutting into squares. These taste even better the next day so try not to eat them all straight away!

Apple Crumble Cake with a Caramel & Apple Icing

◎ **Makes 1 large cake (10–14 slices)**

🕐 **45 minutes**

🍽 **35–40 minutes**

A crumble is one of my favourite desserts, no matter what fruit you use, but this elevated fancy apple crumble cake takes that classic and transforms it to a true showstopper and real centrepiece for special occasions.

250g (9oz) unsalted butter, softened, plus extra for greasing
3 Cox or Granny Smith apples, peeled, cored and cut into smallish cubes
225g (8oz) caster (superfine) sugar, plus 3 tbsp
3 medium free-range eggs
250g (2 cups) self-raising flour
½ tsp baking powder
¼ tsp ground cinnamon

For the crumble top

35g (1¼oz) unsalted butter
50g (2oz) plain (all-purpose) flour
1 heaped tbsp soft light brown sugar
30g (1oz) chopped hazelnuts

For the filling/icing

2 Cox apples, peeled, cored and thinly sliced
30g (1oz) caster (superfine) sugar
250g (9oz) unsalted butter, softened
200g (7oz) dulce de leche/caramel
150g (5oz) icing (confectioner's) sugar

1 Preheat the oven to 170°C/150°C fan/325°F/Gas 3 and grease and line two 20cm (8in) deep sandwich tins with baking parchment.

2 Put the apple cubes into a pan with a splash of water and the 3 tablespoons of sugar. Bring to a simmer and cook gently for 10 minutes or so until they have broken down. Add a little more water as they cook if they look a bit dry. Set aside to cool completely.

3 In a bowl, whisk the softened butter and caster sugar together until light and fluffy. Beat the eggs in one at a time until you have a rich, smooth mixture. Fold in the flour, baking powder and cinnamon, then fold in the cooked apple. If the mixture is a little thick you can add a splash of milk or a dollop of yoghurt.

4 Divide the mixture between the two tins and bake in the centre of the oven for 35–40 minutes until a skewer comes out clean. Cool in the tin for 10 minutes, then turn out onto a wire rack to cool completely. Increase the oven temperature to 180°C/160°C fan/350°F/Gas 4.

5 Make the crumble. Rub the butter and flour together with your fingertips until it forms pea-sized lumps, then stir in the sugar and nuts. Spread over a lined baking sheet and bake for 10–12 minutes until golden. Allow to cool.

6 Make the filling/icing. Put the apples into a pan with the caster sugar and 40g (1½oz) of the butter. Cook gently, stirring occasionally, for 10 minutes until the sugar has melted and the apples are glossy. Increase the heat and bubble for 3–4 minutes until they are caramelised and sticky. Allow to cool.

7   Whisk the rest of the butter with the dulce de leche/caramel
    and the icing sugar until smooth and pillowy. If it seizes, add
    a splash of hot water and whisk until it comes back to a gorgeous,
    smooth consistency.

8   When you are ready to assemble, put one cake on a serving plate.
    Spread over half the icing and add a scattering of the caramelised
    apples and half the crumble, then top with the second cake.
    Spread the other half of the icing over the top and scatter with
    the rest of the caramel apples and crumble.

Favourite Desserts

Chocolate, Hazelnut & Sea Salt Cookies

◎ Makes 12

🕐 20 minutes

🍪 12–14 minutes

Depending on how gooey and chewy you like your cookies you can cook these a little more or less than the time I've given here. You might need to make a couple of batches to find your perfect number but no one will be complaining as these cookies are gloriously moreish!

1 Preheat the oven to 180°C/160°C fan/350°F/Gas 4 and line one large or two smaller baking trays with baking parchment.

2 Put the butter into a pan and melt over a low heat, then allow to cook until it smells lovely and nutty. Pour into a shallow dish or bowl and chill until set but not hard (the consistency of softened butter).

3 Beat the butter with the sugars in a free-standing mixer on a high speed until light and fluffy. This will take about 5 minutes.

4 Stir the flour, salt and bicarbonate of soda together in a medium bowl. Add a little of this flour mix to the butter mixture, add the egg and mix to incorporate the egg. Reduce the speed to low and add the rest of the flour mixture along with the hazelnuts and chocolate.

5 Spoon dollops of the mixture (a small ice-cream scoop works brilliantly here) onto the lined trays, leaving a good amount of space between them as they will spread when they bake. Bake for 12–14 minutes until even and golden. You may need to rotate or turn the trays halfway, depending on your oven.

6 Remove from the oven and sprinkle some flaky sea salt over the cookies. Leave to cool on the trays for at least 5 minutes before devouring.

175g (6oz) unsalted butter
100g (3½oz) caster (superfine) sugar
75g (3oz) light muscovado sugar
200g (1½ cups) self-raising flour
Pinch of sea salt, plus flaky sea salt to scatter
½ tsp bicarbonate of soda (baking soda)
1 large free-range egg, lightly beaten
80g (3¼oz) roughly chopped roasted hazelnuts
80g (3¼oz) dark chocolate, roughly chopped

Sharing Vanilla Panna Cotta with Caramelised Blood Oranges & Rhubarb

◎ Serves 6–8

⏱ 20 minutes, plus setting

🍲 15 minutes

Panna cotta is a dreamy, wobbly Italian dessert that will surprise you as to just how simple it is to make. It's the perfect vehicle for a whole range of toppings like berry compote, baked stone fruit or the winter citrus and rhubarb one here. The amount of gelatine you need will vary from brand to brand – most packet amounts tend to make a firm set so if you like your panna cotta a bit more wibbly reduce the number of leaves by 1 or 2.

Vegetable or rapeseed oil, for greasing
1 litre (4 cups) single cream
60g (2¼oz) caster (superfine) sugar
2 vanilla pods, split and seeds scraped out (or 1 tsp vanilla extract)
Around 10 gelatine leaves, or enough to set 1 litre of liquid (see note in introduction above)

For the caramelised orange and rhubarb

350g (12oz) forced rhubarb, trimmed and cut into 5cm (2in) pieces
4 blood oranges
200g (7oz) caster (superfine) sugar, plus extra for sprinkling
125ml (½ cup) water

1   Preheat the oven to 150°C/130°C fan/300°F/Gas 2 and lightly grease a 1 litre (2 pint) dish with a neutral oil.

2   Put the cream, sugar and vanilla pods and seeds into a pan and place over a medium-high heat. Bring to a gentle simmer and stir until the sugar has dissolved, then remove from the heat.

3   Meanwhile, soak the gelatine leaves in cold water for 5 minutes until very soft and floppy, then squeeze out any excess water.

4   Remove and discard the vanilla pods from the warmed cream, then add the softened gelatine and stir through until dissolved. Pour the mix into the prepared dish and set aside in the fridge to set for 2 hours or overnight to set completely.

5   Put the rhubarb pieces into a roasting tray so they fit snugly. Squeeze over the juice of one of the blood oranges and a sprinkle of sugar then cover with foil and roast for 15 minutes until they are just tender but not falling apart. Leave to cool then pour off any of the juice into a jug. Top the rhubarb juice up to 125ml (½ cup) with hot water.

6   Cut the skin and all the pith off from the other oranges and slice into thin rounds. Put into a bowl with the cooled rhubarb.

7   Put the sugar into a heavy-based pan with 125ml (½ cup) water. Place over a low heat and allow the sugar to melt, then increase the heat and bring to the boil. Bubble until you have a dark, deep caramel. Remove from the heat and carefully pour the rhubarb juice and water mixture into the deep caramel. It will splutter and hiss but that is normal. Swirl until you have a smooth sauce and pour this over the rhubarb and oranges.

8   Serve the caramelised oranges and rhubarb on top of the
     panna cotta.

Perfect Fruit Galette

◎ Serves 6–8

⬚ 1 hour, plus chilling

⬓ 30–35 minutes

A truly stunning galette that is perfect made with summer fruits. You can skip the frangipane if you want to simplify the recipe slightly but it does add a fairly irresistible sweet and indulgent layer. The rough puff pastry has a high butter content so you need to cook this tart at a high temperature. If some of the butter leaks out while baking don't panic; it will still be utterly delicious.

250g (2 cups) plain
  (all-purpose) flour
1 tsp caster (superfine) sugar
Good pinch of sea salt
160g (5½oz) unsalted butter,
  frozen for at least 1 hour
3 medium free-range eggs,
  1 beaten for glazing
1 tsp cider vinegar
80ml (⅓ cup) ice-cold water
6 ripe peaches
125g (4oz) blueberries
1 tbsp demerara sugar
3 tbsp apricot jam
Lightly whipped cream or crème
  fraîche, to serve

For the frangipane

100g (3½oz) unsalted butter,
  softened
100g (3½oz) caster (superfine)
  sugar
2 medium free-range eggs
100g (3½oz) ground almonds
25g (1oz) plain (all-purpose) flour

1 Put the flour, sugar and salt in a large bowl and, using a box grater, coarsely grate the frozen butter into the bowl and toss to coat the strands in the flour. In a measuring jug, whisk together 2 of the eggs, vinegar and cold water until combined. Make a well in the centre of the flour and butter mixture and pour in the liquid.

2 Using two large forks, gently toss all the ingredients together until the dough takes shape and begins to hold together. Turn the dough out and bring together quickly with your hands and shape into a disc. Wrap in cling film and chill for half an hour.

3 Preheat the oven to 210°C/190°C fan/410°F/Gas 7 and line a large baking sheet with baking parchment. Roll out the pastry on a lightly floured surface to form a 40cm (16in) circle, then slide onto the lined baking sheet. Chill in the fridge while you make the frangipane.

4 In a separate bowl, beat together the butter and sugar until light and fluffy. Whisk in the eggs one at a time and then fold through the ground almonds and flour. Spread this mixture across the base of the pastry, leaving a 5cm (2in) border around the outside. Return to the fridge while you prepare the peaches.

5 Halve and remove the stones and then slice each half into 4 wedges. Arrange these in concentric circles on top of the frangipane so they stick up out of the almond mixture. Scatter all over with the blueberries.

6   Bring the edges of the pastry up and in and crimp into a pretty wheel around the outer layer of peaches. Brush the pastry edges all over with the beaten egg and then scatter all over with the demerara sugar.

7   Bake the tart for 30–35 minutes, or until the frangipane and pastry are golden brown. Remove the tart from the oven and allow to cool until just warm. Melt the apricot jam with a tiny splash of water in a pan then strain to make a smooth glaze. Brush this all over the fruit so it glistens, then serve with lightly whipped cream or crème fraîche.

Buttery Cinnamon Bun Tray Bake

◎ Makes 12

⏱ 2 hours, plus proving

🍲 15 minutes

These make an amazing breakfast. If you want to do an overnight dough, cover and chill once they are in the baking tin. The next morning remove from the fridge and allow to sit in a warm place for an hour until puffy before baking. If you do have any left over you can wrap in foil and then warm through the next day.

80g (3 ¼ oz) unsalted butter
250ml (1 cup) whole milk
500g (4 cups) strong white
    bread flour
1 × 7g (¼oz) sachet of
    fast-action yeast
50g (2oz) caster (superfine) sugar
1 tsp fine sea salt
2 tsp ground cardamom
1 large free-range egg plus 1 large
    yolk, beaten together
1 beaten egg, for glazing
1 tbsp demerara sugar

For the filling

150g (5oz) unsalted butter, softened
100g (3½oz) soft light brown sugar
2 tbsp ground cinnamon

1   Gently melt the butter and milk together in a pan over a low heat until the butter has melted. Set aside until lukewarm (about 40°C/100°F).

2   Mix the flour, yeast, caster sugar, salt and cardamom together in a large bowl. Make a well in the centre and pour in the beaten egg and yolk followed by the warm milk and butter mixture. Use a wooden spoon to mix until you have a slightly sticky dough.

3   When the dough has taken shape, turn out onto a floured surface and knead for about 10 minutes until smooth and springy. (Alternatively knead in a stand mixer with a dough hook for 4–5 minutes.) Dust with flour if you find the dough too sticky.

4   Transfer the dough to a clean greased bowl, cover with a damp tea towel and let it rise in a warm place for 1 hour, or until it has doubled in size.

5   For the filling, beat all the ingredients in a bowl until you have a smooth paste.

6   When the dough has risen, punch it down in the bowl and tip onto a lightly greased work surface. Roll into a rectangle 45 x 30cm (17 x 12in) and about 5mm (¼in) thick. Spread the filling all over and then, starting from one long side, roll the dough into a cylinder. Use a sharp knife to slice into 12 equal-sized pieces.

7   Lightly grease a roasting tray that is about 25 x 20cm (10 x 8in) and place the rolls in cut-side up. Cover with lightly greased cling film and leave to rise for 30–40 minutes in a warm place until puffy.

8   Preheat the oven to 200°C/180° fan/400°F/Gas 6. Brush the buns with the egg, sprinkle with the sugar and bake for 15 minutes, or until golden brown.

9   Leave the buns to cool in the tin for 10 minutes, then transfer to a wire rack to cool a little before serving.

Favourite Desserts

Irish Tea Cake (Barmbrack)

Make 1 large loaf

🍶 30 minutes, plus soaking

🍳 1¼–1½ hours

Finding the ring in a slice of barmbrack always garnered huge excitement in our school lunchroom growing up. This rich and moist tea cake is a classic Irish bake that is traditionally made around Halloween and should you choose to bake a ring into the batter, the lucky person who gets it in their slice is next to be married!

1 Put the dried fruit into a bowl, pour over the tea and whiskey and leave to soak for at least 4 hours or overnight.

2 Preheat the oven to 170°C/150°C fan/325°F/Gas 3 and grease and line a 900ml (2lb) loaf tin with baking parchment. Stir the mixed peel and almonds into the soaked fruit and set aside.

3 Whisk the flour, sugar, baking powder, mixed spice and salt together in a large bowl. Stir in the beaten egg and the soaked fruit mixture. Dollop into the prepared tin and bake for 1¼–1½ hours, or until a skewer comes out clean. Check after 1 hour; if it is going too dark on top you can cover it with a piece of foil. Once cooked, allow to cool in the tin for 30 minutes, then turn onto a wire rack.

4 Put the sugar and 3 tablespoons water into a small pan over a low heat. Once the sugar has melted bring to the boil and bubble until you have a light syrup.

5 Brush the barmbrack all over with this sticky glaze and allow to cool completely. Store overnight in an airtight container to allow the flavours to develop before slicing and serving, either as it is or toasted with butter.

50g (2oz) currants
150g (5oz) sultanas (golden raisins)
150g (5oz) raisins
50g (2oz) prunes, chopped
300ml (1¼ cups) strong tea, cooled a little
4 tbsp Irish whiskey
50g (2oz) mixed peel, roughly chopped
40g (1½ oz) flaked almonds
200g (1½ cups) plain (all-purpose) flour
130g (4½oz) soft light brown sugar
2 tsp baking powder
1 tsp mixed spice
Good pinch of salt
1 medium free-range egg, beaten
2 tbsp caster (superfine) sugar

The Perfect Funfetti Birthday Cake

◎ Makes 20 squares

🫙 15 minutes

🍲 30 minutes

It might seem weird to add boiling water to icing but trust me –
it makes for the smoothest, fluffiest icing imaginable. Once you try
this method you won't turn back.

400g (14oz) unsalted butter,
softened
350g (12oz) caster (superfine) sugar
400g (14oz) free-range eggs
(weighed in their shells)
2 tsp vanilla bean paste
400g (3 cups) plain (all-purpose)
flour
1 tbsp baking powder
300ml (1¼ cups) buttermilk
or natural yoghurt
80g (3¼oz) large sugar sprinkles

For the icing

200g (7oz) unsalted butter, softened
300g 10oz) icing (confectioner's)
sugar
2 tsp vanilla bean paste
Pink food colouring
1–2 tbsp just-boiled water
Sprinkles, to decorate

1   Preheat the oven to 200°C/180°C fan/400°F/Gas 6 and grease
and line a 33 x 23cm (13 x 9in) baking tray or cake tin.

2   Cream the butter and sugar together until light and fluffy.
Gradually add the eggs and vanilla bean paste, mixing well
between each addition.

3   Gently fold in one-third of the flour, the baking powder
and one-third of the buttermilk or yoghurt; repeat until you
have added all of the flour and buttermilk.

4   Fold in the sprinkles, then spoon the batter into the prepared
tin and smooth until level. Bake for 30 minutes until risen and
lightly golden and a skewer inserted in the centre comes out
clean. Cool in the tin for 5–10 minutes, then turn out onto
a wire rack to cool completely.

5   Meanwhile make the icing. Beat the butter until light and
fluffy then gradually beat in the icing sugar until you have a
smooth icing. Add the vanilla bean paste, food colouring and
1–2 tablespoons of just-boiled water. Whisk together to make
a bright, smooth icing.

6   Once the cake is cool, transfer to a serving plate or board.
Spread the icing all over the cake with a swirly pattern
then scatter with the sprinkles and serve.

INDEX

ACKNOWLEDGEMENTS

Thank you lovely reader for cooking up a storm and making this cookbook part of your collection, I hope it brings you plenty of great meals and delicious dinners.

To Sofie, for keeping the show on the road and for the love you bring to our little world despite all the madness! From roadside edit meltdowns to finishing books in hotel rooms, can you believe you got me through ten of these? You have the patience of a saint!

Our little dudes, Noah and Ollie for always being adventurous and excited about what ends up on the kitchen table! You make cooking even more exciting and I love it all the more with you both in our world.

To my very fabulous food editor Lizzie Kamenetzky, for helping mould my wild food ideas into the very manageable recipes you see on the pages of this book, thank you for helping me put the final and considered seasoning into yet another cookbook.

My A-Team at United Agents: Rosemary Scoular and Aoife Rice. Thank you both for keeping a clear steer on everything we do and particularly your wise guidance on so many aspects of what we do including this book.

To Sarah-Kim Watchorn, for your beautiful food styling throughout the pages of this book and for helping make so many of my recipes come to life. To Susan Willis for cooking through so many of the recipes in the book throughout the shoot – don't mention the peaches, mup in the crush!

To Liz Gough and Issy Gonzalez-Prendergast for taking me on for number ten and helping shape this into the book it is! To our brilliant little team at Hodder in the UK: Olivia Nightingall, Alice Morley and Vero Norton.

Thank you Evi O. for helping us shape a whole new look and feel with your striking design and art direction.

To Evan Doherty for shooting a fresh new look for the cover. Thanks for bringing new life to the only blue steel I have to offer!

To Clare Sayer for crossing the 't's and dotting the 'i's, thank you for making everything just right.

To Brian Walsh at RTÉ, for guidance through another TV project, your vision helps shape our shows so a big thank you!

To Suzanne Weldon and Helen Sommerville and all of the SPAR crew who have supported me from day one.

To my very brilliant assistant Kate Dowling, thanks for keeping the show on the road and keeping me on my toes!

To our brilliant team at our production company, Appetite Media. Robin Murray, Marc Dillon, Faye Williamson, Dee Savage, Paul Kehoe, Chloe Chan, Ross Bradshaw, Patrick Corr, Alex Lynch, Barry Morey, Oliver Kelly, Rory Bradley, Michael Boyle & all of our brilliant editors for bringing the recipes in this book to life so beautifully in the accompanying TV series.

Finally, thank you to my family and friends, who are regular guinea pigs for all the recipes!